the girl's guide
to life on
two wheels

the girl's guide
to life on
two wheels

Cathy Bussey

LONDON • NEW YORK

For the little ones in my life: Ethan, Neve, Lily, Cherry, and William, who joined them just in the nick of time! And for whoever follows…

Design Carl Hodson and Maria Lee-Warren
Editor Rebecca Woods
Production Toby Marshall
Art Director Leslie Harrington
Editorial Director Julia Charles

Ilustrations Qian Wu and Chloe True
Indexer Sandra Shotter

First published in 2013 by
Ryland Peters & Small
20–21 Jockey's Fields
London WC1R 4BW
and
519 Broadway, 5th Floor
New York, NY 10012

www.rylandpeters.com

10 9 8 7 6 5 4 3 2 1

Text © Cathy Bussey 2013
Design and illustrations © Ryland Peters & Small 2013
Full photography credits on page 128

Printed in China

ISBN: 978-1-84975-371-5

A CIP record for this book is available from the British Library.

US Library of Congress CIP data has been applied for.

Introduction

2012 was an incredible year for cycling. The performance of leading female cyclists Victoria Pendleton, Kristin Armstrong, Laura Trott, Lizzie Armitstead, Dani King, Joanna Rowsell and Sarah Storey saw the sport capture the imagination of women like never before.

2012 was the icing on the cake, because there has been a buzz around women's cycling for many years now. Golden girls like Victoria Pendleton and Kristin Armstrong have led the charge, but the movement is as embedded in grass roots as it is on the international stage.

Cycling has inspired fashion designers, artists and photographers. The innate elegance and style of a woman on a bike has a timeless appeal. And unlike many sports and hobbies that require a big budget or a massive time commitment, cycling is accessible to just about anyone.

Once upon a time cycling was dominated by men, on the international stage and at grass-roots level. This was reflected in the range of bicycles and accessories available on the market.

Thankfully, the tide has turned. Retailers, designers and manufacturers have switched on to the fact that women want to cycle, big time. They have also switched on to the fact that many women want to cycle without compromising their own personal style. As Victoria Pendleton herself told the *Daily Telegraph*: 'Most women don't want to squeeze into Lycra before they jump on a bike.'

And they no longer have to. A whole new world of stylish and fashionable cycling clothes and accessories has sprung up to accompany the growing interest in cycling among women.

The Girl's Guide to Life on Two Wheels is for any woman who wants to cycle, at any level. The social, economical and personal reasons for cycling are many and varied. Cycling is fun, environmentally friendly, budget friendly, fashion friendly and just friendly, full stop.

Cycling is also a relatively small life change that can make a huge difference. In the course of researching this book, I have spoken to many women about the positive impact cycling has had upon their lives and some of their testimonies are reproduced in these pages. The overwhelming message I received is that choosing to start cycling was one of the best decisions they ever made.

Victoria Pendleton summed it up beautifully at the launch of the UK women-only cycling event Cycletta when she said: 'I want to inspire women to join me and cycle; as a hobby, a sport, a way to get fit and healthy. Whatever the reasoning, cycling can improve your life.'

Whether you are considering getting back on your bike for the first time since childhood, or thinking about starting to learn to cycle, I hope that the information and inspiration contained within this book will help you take the decision to start your own cycling journey.

My cycling journey

As a child and then a teenager I cycled everywhere. Public transport was scarce in the small village I grew up in, so cycling simply made sense. But once I passed my driving test, my bike was cast aside as the novelty of hurtling everywhere in a car became more appealing. Then came university and a career, and cycling dropped off the radar for me for many years. Thinking back, there was no obvious reason. I simply never thought to cycle and instead walked, drove or took public transport. At the same time I was wasting hours – and money – at the gym, running, cross-training and stepping nowhere in a boring air-conditioned room, gazing blankly at MTV while wondering how quickly I could finish up and drive – yes drive! – home.

It was only once I moved to London that I changed my outlook. I started noticing cyclists far more. I would heave myself onto packed trains to spend a tedious, uncomfortable, overheated hour travelling to work. All around me, people were whizzing into work in half that time on bikes. But still the penny didn't drop for me. Cycling to work was what 'other people' did. I simply assumed I 'couldn't' cycle. It was too far, I didn't own a bike, I didn't want to arrive at work sweaty and red in the face, I didn't have time, I didn't have any of the gear; the list of excuses went on. 'I'd love to cycle,' I'd say regretfully, 'but I can't…'

Then one day my boyfriend, who had been commuting to work by bike for two years, went away for a few days and left me his bike and an A–Z of London with the route to work drawn on it. An experimental cycle proved that the saying 'it's like riding a bike' exists for a reason. It was like I had never stopped cycling. The instincts, ability and skills required to cycle safely were firmly ingrained and I was able to draw upon them straight away.

I cycled to work the very next day. It took me 50 minutes to travel six miles and I had to stop every three minutes or so to check the map. The sense of achievement and accomplishment when I arrived was unbelievable. I remember showering and changing and sitting down at my desk, fresh, wide awake and energized. I looked at yawning, groggy colleagues who had sleepwalked from the train to the office and wondered, why isn't everyone doing this? On payday, I tore up my travel card, marched straight to the nearest bike shop and left the proud owner of the cheapest, most basic and to me the most beautiful bike in the world.

I loved everything about cycling – the freedom, the independence, the money-saving aspects, the feeling of accomplishment and the effect it had on my fitness and figure. But on the face of it, despite its many enthusiastic and high-profile advocates, the very act of cycling itself did not seem to be the pursuit of the fashion forward. Not that I consider myself fashion forward in the slightest, but even I baulked at the conventional

Below: As soon as I saw this gorgeous pink Pashley Poppy I fell madly in love with it. This is my 'for special occasions' bike – it's far too beautiful to use for the daily commute.

'cycling gear' on offer. Clothing was skintight, hi-vis or Lycra – sometimes all three. Accessories were either black, grey or dark blue – typically no-frills, no-nonsense colours. The only cycling bags on offer were sturdy, tough rucksacks or grey panniers. Everything out there seemed to be aimed at men, and specifically men who also purchased ludicrously expensive carbon-framed bikes, yellow jerseys and something called 'wet lube'.

Then one day I read a newspaper article that literally changed my life. Iconic UK fashion destination Topshop was to start selling women's designer cycling accessories. It had never occurred to me that such a concept could exist. I went on a mammoth search and discovered a whole new dimension to cycling.

It isn't just fun and practical: cycling is inherently stylish. I discovered there were dedicated online stores selling beautiful, well-made products for female cyclists. There were ladies-only cycling events and fundraisers, charity bike events, even overnight coastal rides. There were fashion designers building entire collections around cycling. I clearly wasn't the only one who had rediscovered my love of all things two-wheeled. Cycling was literally in *Vogue*.

We have come a full, perfect circle. Cycling occupies its rightful place – once again it is stylish and fashionable, liberating and empowering.

If you are thinking about starting cycling, or know someone who is thinking about cycling, this book is here to help. It will address common perceptions about cycling and show you how you can cycle safely and, if you want, stylishly. It will, I hope, inspire you and motivate you to give cycling a go. It will give you information on how to choose a bike, how to look after your bike and what to do if you get a puncture. It will give you ideas on how to incorporate cycling into your everyday routine and keep you motivated if on a cold rainy winter's day you are feeling a bit so-so

Above: Here I am posing happily with my trusty Pinnacle hybrid bike, to which, I freely admit, I am very emotionally attached.

about it all. It will offer inspiring advice from high-profile cyclists and will help you get the most from the growing cycling scene – how it can boost your social life as well as your fitness and bank balance. If you are anything like the many women who have helped inform this book, you will find that turning to two wheels will be one of the best things you ever do.

I will leave you with a word of warning – cycling is completely addictive. When you have reached the stage where you persuade yourself you need two bikes, one for everyday and one for special occasions, you'll know you've got the cycling bug.

why
cycle?

1

In case you hadn't been paying attention, there's been a bit of a revolution going on around you...

Whether you've vaguely registered that some incredibly talented women have been scooping gold medals on the global stage or idly commented on how many bikes you're seeing on the roads now, chances are you've noticed there are a lot more women on two wheels than there used to be. Women's cycling is back, and in a big way.

Cycling has been empowering women since the 19th century. The humble bicycle set our great-great-grandmothers free, giving them an independence they had previously only dreamed of. It reduced the need for their ubiquitous male chaperones. It released them from their ludicrously hot, heavy, restrictive attire, including corsets, floor-length skirts and gigantic knickers. Cycling became synonymous with women's equality, with the movement for suffrage and with the notion that women simply would no longer fade into the shadows.

Below: The bicycle – officially empowering women and representing independence, intelligence and style since the 19th century.

Today, even with all the options and choices for transport and fitness available to us – which for a time seemed so much more appealing – more and more women are discovering a new freedom through cycling. And when you think about it, it makes perfect sense. Cycling is a great way to get to any destination. We all travel in our daily lives and jumping on a bike offers one of the best forms of exercise and transport there is. It is quick, cheap, healthy and very environmentally friendly. It also gives you a sense of independence and freedom you just cannot get from any other form of transport.

There are few women out there who have literally never been on a bike in their lives. But if that's you, the good news is, it's never too late to learn. For many of us, our bike was our only transport when we were young. Then lifts from parents, the bus, the train or our own car seemed an easier and more practical option.

But once you think about it, are these other forms of transport really so attractive? Cars are expensive and

polluting, and traffic jams are now practically unavoidable. Buses are slow, crowded, overheated in summer and freezing in winter. Trains, tubes and metros are jam-packed with stressed, irritable commuters. If you are reliant on somebody else for lifts, you are at the mercy of their schedule. Crucially, none of these forms of transport can help you glow with health, de-stress and tone those hard-to-reach areas like thighs and bums. Reading this thinking: 'But I walk everywhere, that's how I stay active'? You'll feel, and see, far more benefits from cycling and you'll get about a lot quicker too.

There are more cyclists on the roads than ever before and the bike is replacing the car as the ultimate form of transport. A combination of a squeezed economic climate, an increased awareness of the impact of transport on the environment, the inherent fashion and style credentials of the bicycle and an increasing concern about our very sedentary lifestyles has motivated many to take to two wheels. Quick, efficient, affordable, healthy and environmentally friendly – what's not to love? Why aren't we all doing it? If it's good enough for fashion doyenne

Vivienne Westwood, who chooses a gorgeous vintage Pashley for getting from A to B, then surely it is good enough for the rest of us. As the fashion legend herself told *thelondonpaper*: 'It's convenient and the quickest way to get around. Sometimes I carry high heels in the basket if I'm going somewhere where I'll be needing them.' That 'somewhere' includes film premieres – Vivienne cycled to the premiere of eco-movie *The Age of Stupid* dressed in a fabulous full-length dress.

And Vivienne's not the only member of the fash pack taking to two wheels. Model Agyness Deyn is famed for using her bike to zip between shows at New York Fashion Week. Hollywood star Naomi Watts has been spotted out and about in New York on her bike with son Alexander on the back. *Buffy the Vampire Slayer* star Sarah Michelle Gellar has been photographed with a pink vintage bicycle that has its own devoted online following. The list of celebrities on two wheels goes on and on.

But before we get all celeb-spotter magazine, let's also consider some of the incredible women that have truly shone on the international cycling stage.

Why I cycle

'I'd often felt envious of those who cycled for their daring and their ability to get where they wanted to go without being at the mercy of public transport. A strike on the London Underground finally gave me the push I needed. I cycle primarily for transport, but also for fitness. I love being able to get to where I need to be and knowing exactly how long it's going to take me. I love the toned thighs. It also clears my head and helps me work things out. Finally, cycling is a sign of independence and intelligence – which is always stylish in my opinion.' - Laura, 33

> *'It's convenient and the quickest way to get around. Sometimes I carry high heels in the basket if I'm going somewhere where I'll be needing them.'* – Vivienne Westwood

Top right: Vivienne Westwood arrives at a film premiere in style. Everybody who's anybody has been papped out and about on their bike – cementing cycling's high-fashion credentials.

This page: The incredible Victoria Pendleton races Anna Mears in her final appearance at the London 2012 Velodrome.

'Queen' Victoria Pendleton, the British Olympic gold medallist, has been instrumental in raising the profile of women's cycling in the UK and around the world, along with her fellow Olympians Laura Trott, Lizzie Armitstead, Dani King and Joanna Rowsell. Continuing cycling's glorious tradition of empowering women and putting them on an equal footing with their male counterparts, the cycling women of Team GB practically took a clean sweep at London 2012, leaving behind any nonsense about cycling being

a 'man's sport' and men's cycling being 'more exciting'. Team GB's women were denied gold in very few cycling events – most notably the time trial that saw US cycling legend Kristin Armstrong, the double gold medallist, secure the top honour for a second time. Thirty-eight-year-old Kristin, a mother of two, was also crowned the world time trial champion in 2009. Alongside Victoria Pendleton, she is probably and justifiably the most famous female cyclist in the world and an inspirational role model for female cyclists

Cycling and me

Dani King, women's team pursuit Olympic champion and world record holder

Dani King is part of the next generation of leading UK female cyclists and along with Laura Trott and Joanna Rowsell struck gold at the London Olympics.

'There are many things I love about cycling. First of all, I like to be outside training, especially when the weather is good or I'm riding around roads that are new to me. It can be a great way to train and get fit with friends.

'Since I started riding full time, cycling has been the main focus of my life. My whole year is planned around my training and race programme, and it has to be my priority. Without a doubt, my best achievement so far is my Olympic gold medal – what made it extra special was a home crowd and a world record.

'Like most people who train full time, I can find it difficult to get myself out of the door when I'm feeling tired from previous sessions. The area I struggle most with is lone riding. Some people are perfectly happy with their own company, but I find it difficult to motivate myself if I have a long ride ahead and don't have anybody to ride with. I remind myself of the bigger picture, and how lucky I am to be in a position to train full time.

'Cycling is a great activity. You can meet new friends, get fit and stay healthy at the same time.'

everywhere. Who wouldn't want a part of the world these amazing women inhabit?

Despite all this good news, the wider picture remains that while numbers of cyclists are increasing overall, the increase is still far greater among men than it is women. Today, men are statistically far more likely to cycle than women. There are numerous reasons for this, and we will look at them throughout this book. The truth is that the barriers to cycling that seem so

insurmountable are easily broken down. Very few women 'can't' cycle. The wonderful thing about cycling is that just about anyone can do it, including many people with disabilities. The inspirational men and women of the London 2012 Paralympic Games proved that beyond any doubt. Often all that is needed is a gentle push to give cycling a go. You will feel the benefits immediately and actually see the benefits not long after. And you will quickly find that cycling is truly addictive.

But....! 10 reasons why women are put off cycling

Whatever your situation, there is a way to incorporate cycling into your life, so forget those excuses. Stop telling yourself that you 'can't' and instead start thinking about how you can.

1 *'I don't have time'*

Here's the thing about cycling – it saves you time. It's quicker to cycle to the shops than it is to walk or crawl through traffic. It's quicker to go for a bike ride than it is to drive to the gym and spend 40 minutes working out. It's quicker to cycle through a busy city than it is to walk, take the train or drive. It's quicker to cycle in the countryside than it is to wait for a bus. It may well be quicker for you to cycle to work than it is to take another form of transport.

Cycling is an investment in yourself. It's an investment in your physical and mental health, fitness and wellness. If that's not an investment worth making, I don't know what is. Make time for yourself. Swap an hour on the sofa in front of the TV for an hour's cycle. No matter how tired you think are, you will feel far, far better for it.

2 *'I'm too unfit to cycle. I want to build up my fitness and lose some weight first'*

The best way to get fit enough to cycle, is to cycle. You can start off as slowly as you like. No one will be timing you, judging you or watching you. Start with very short journeys and build up your distances gradually. Your fitness will improve very quickly. Cycling is a low-impact form of exercise: you will burn heaps of calories without the jarring effect on your joints that other aerobic exercise, such as running, can have. Plus it can burn in excess of 500 calories an hour, which is more than you will burn during an hour's walking or swimming. It's the perfect way to get in shape. If you need that extra motivation, sign up for a cycling event to give you a goal to work towards.

It's important to look after your legs and back, and in Chapter Four we will look at some basic stretches and exercises to keep your body fit for your bike.

3 '*The traffic is terrible where I live*'

Traffic is a fact of life. If you live in a city, or you cycle during busy commuting hours, you will have to learn to cope with traffic. There is a raft of help available and cycling on busy roads is not as difficult as it sounds. Often the major barrier is confidence. A few sessions with a cycling instructor will help you learn to handle traffic and cycle confidently on even the busiest of roads. You can also look up alternative routes, avoiding main highways and sticking to smaller, quieter roads, off-road tracks and cycle paths.

4 '*Isn't cycling dangerous?*'

Let's look at the statistics. In 2011, according to the Royal Society for the Prevention of Accidents, there were just over 19,000 reported accidents involving cyclists in the UK. Of these, 107 involved fatalities and 3,085 involved serious injuries, with the vast majority – 16,023 – involving slight injuries.

Considering that a report by the London School of Economics estimated the number of cyclists in the UK in 2010 to stand at a whopping 13 million, the chances of an accident, although real, start to look very small. In 2011, ROSPA also reported that there were 203,000 accidents involving motorists. Clearly, the number of motorists vastly outnumbers that of cyclists, but would any of us argue that travelling by car is 'dangerous', even when there is far more risk of being involved in an accident based on numbers alone?

The figures for the US tell a similar story. According to National Highway Traffic Safety Administration data, in 2010 there were 618 cycling fatalities and 52,000 cycling injuries. This represents a drop from 2009 when there were 630 cycling fatalities, and a significant drop from the 830 cycling fatalities in 1995.

There is risk associated with everything we do. No form of transport is 100 per cent risk free; but then, nothing in life is 100 per cent risk free. Accidents do happen and they can have tragic consequences, but that in itself is no more a reason not to cycle than it is a reason not to drive, get the train or take the bus. In fact, the more cyclists there are on the roads, the safer cycling becomes, as motorists and other road users learn to look out for cyclists.

5 *'I have children'*

Get them cycling too! Cycling is a very family-friendly hobby and children pick up the ability to cycle very quickly – after all, most of us would have learned as a child. Cycle the children to school in the morning or go for family bike rides after school and at weekends. It's a great way to get your figure back after pregnancy too. You can buy baby seats that fit securely to the back of your bike for transporting little ones, and there are even attachments to allow you to tow toddlers along on their own mini-bikes or in trailers.

If you don't fancy putting your baby on the back of your bike, use the time you spend cycling as valuable 'me time' to de-stress and temporarily forget about the responsibilities of parenthood – just for half an hour!

Below: Cycling is incredibly family friendly and it's a great way to get around with your little ones and help you get your figure back after pregnancy.

6 '**I am worried about looking stupid**'

If you don't want your partner, friends or family to see you on your bike until you have built up your confidence, practise in a quiet spot on your own until you are ready to cycle with other people. If you are worried about looking silly in front of other cyclists and road users – why do you care what a bunch of strangers think of you? And when did you last look at a cyclist and think 'Wow, they look stupid?' Never. So why would anyone think that about you?

I mean this in the nicest way possible – nobody is going to be looking at you, criticizing you or judging you, because the only person who really cares what you look like is you. We worry far too much about what other people think of us, and what we look like to them. But everybody else is too busy worrying about themselves to really pay much attention to you!

7 '**The weather is too unpredictable for cycling**'

Dress for the weather and always carry a light waterproof jacket in your bag in case of an unexpected downpour. Yes, sometimes it is cold, windy and wet, but that's what warm fleeces, gloves and waterproof jackets are for. Check out Chapter 4, Cycling in All Seasons, for some smart ways to keep out the chill while on your bike. And just remember, there's nothing nicer than coming back to a hot bath in a warm house after a brisk cycle in the winter air. You'll be glowing on the inside as well as the outside.

8 '**I don't want to spend all my time fixing punctures**'

Punctures are by no means an everyday occurrence. And when they do occur, repairing a punctured tyre is really not as hard or as arduous as it sounds – it's a five-minute job and we'll look at basic maintenance in Chapter 6, Keeping Your Bike Healthy.

If you really want to keep your time spent with a spanner to a minimum, invest in some of the brilliant technology available such as Slime self-healing inner tubes or puncture-resistant Kevlar tyres. Alternatively, just pop into your local bike shop and let the experts do the hard work for you.

9 ‘I don't want to arrive at my destination all hot and sweaty’

If you're cycling to work, many offices are now kitted out with showers for employees who cycle. If yours is not or you are cycling somewhere without a shower you can quickly leap into, plan ahead. Invest in extra-strength deodorant and cycling gear made from sweat-wicking fabrics (see Chapter Four, Cycling in All Seasons) to keep you fresh and dry. Take it easy the last mile or two to give yourself time to cool down. Pack deodorant, wipes and a change of top. Allow yourself five minutes to freshen up in the cloakroom before you officially arrive.

10 ‘No one looks good in Lycra’

There is no law that says cycling and Lycra must go hand in hand. As we will discover in Chapter Five, Looking Good While Cycling, there is an entire movement dedicated to beautiful and practical cycling gear and accessories that offers so much choice, you might find yourself wondering what to wear just to get on your bike!

Why I cycle

‘I started cycling about five years ago, going for long rides in the countryside as a way to get exercise and enjoy the scenery. Cycling is really important to me. It's my favoured method of travel, getting fit and seeing the world. Sometimes if I feel like I'm too tired to cycle to work I get the bus. That's when I remember it takes me twice as long and I always, always regret it and wish I'd cycled.’ – Lou, 32

Left: It's perfectly possible to look fantastic on two wheels, with not an inch of Lycra in sight.

This page: There's no better way to explore the countryside than by bike.

2

choosing a bike

Bikes come in all kinds of wonderful styles, sizes and shades. There really is something for everybody.

Your bike needs to be functional enough to get you from A to B, but also think about what you want the bike to say about you. A bike is as much an accessory as a car, a handbag or a pair of shoes. You need to love your bike. If you love it, you'll use it more often, take better care of it and invest more in it. Your bike should make you smile, make you proud and make you want to leap aboard. Ultimately, if you have your heart set on a certain type of bike – a vintage shopper, a speedy road bike, a hip fixie – you can probably adapt it to suit your lifestyle.

Left and above: Whatever your style, there's a bike out there to suit you.

Types of bike

Mountain bikes

Mountain bikes are the 4 x 4s of the bike world, but without the unethical 'gas guzzling' implications. Tough and practical rather than super-speedy, they have wide, thick grippy tyres that can withstand all but the most severe of punctures. Mountain bikes have chunky frames, excellent brakes and more gears than may be considered reasonably necessary. Some come with suspension, which can add weight but ensures a smooth ride when bouncing over bumpy surfaces.

Pros
Hard wearing, suitable for off-roading and general bouncing around, not prone to punctures, fairly affordable and low maintenance.

Cons
Thick tyres really do slow these bikes down on smooth surfaces. Can be cumbersome and heavy.

Road bikes

The Porsches of the bike world, road bikes are sleek, compact and light, with characteristic dropped handlebars. Tyres are thin and slick, which make a road-based commute lightning quick. The main selling point of the road bike is their speed. They are the fastest bikes on the block by a long shot and those who ride them swear by them.

On the flip side, their super-thin tyres are prone to punctures and the wheels are delicate – you wouldn't want to take a road bike down a bumpy path for fear of buckling a wheel. They are also a little flimsy and unstable, which can make novices uncomfortable.

Pros
Fast, fast, fast! Lightweight and compact.

Cons
Prone to punctures, wheels are not very strong, expensive, fairly high maintenance, may not be suitable for complete beginners.

Touring bikes

To the untrained eye, touring bikes and road bikes are pretty much one and the same. They have similar frames, but touring bikes have a slightly rangier, sturdier, more stable build. The tyres are a little wider and they are built for long-distance comfort, not short-distance speed. Touring bikes may also have more gears than road bikes, as they are built for a range of terrain. They are, however, nowhere near as hardy as mountain bikes. Sticking with the car theme, touring bikes are your Mercedes saloons – combining high performance with comfort.

Pros
Comfortable, smooth, built to last.

Cons
Can be expensive, not suitable for off-roading, performance rather than style orientated.

Hybrid bikes

Billed as the best of both worlds, hybrid bikes bring together the robust toughness of mountain bikes with the speed credentials of road bikes. Hybrids range from very slender, almost racing-style bikes with flat handlebars to chunky mountain bike-style models with slick tyres. If a hybrid bike were a car, it would be a mid-range saloon or coupe. Practical, affordable and still eminently lovable.

Pros

Stronger than a road bike, faster than a mountain bike. Ideal for commuting and recreational cycling.

Cons

Jack of all trades but master of none – hybrids are not as fast as road or touring bikes, as tough as bouncy mountain bikes or as gorgeous as some of the vintage-style 'sit up and beg' models.

Folding bikes

Folding bikes are a familiar sight in commuterville. These cute little numbers fold up nice and small, making them ideal for train journeys and for storage in small flats. Unfold them and – hey presto – you have a fully functioning, adorably quirky-looking bike. Folding bikes are not cheap, but considering they can be taken pretty much anywhere and are virtually theft proof, those who own them consider the investment well worth it. I can't think of a car analogy for a folding bike, as how many cars do you know that fold up?

Pros

Small and versatile, functional, practical, can be stored just about anywhere, practically theft proof.

Cons

Designed for the urban commuter, these bikes are not the best choice for purely recreational cycling. Can be pricey.

Shoppers

Also known as Dutch or 'sit up and beg' bikes, these beauties are characterized by their stunning style and design. They have low, curved bars, few gears, high-set handlebars – which practically beg you to fit a basket to them – and large, comfortable saddles. These bikes are the vintage classics of the bicycle world and are ideal for travelling elegantly. They scream femininity and just looking at them conjures up images of cycling through summer meadows for lazy picnics, or cruising through town with flowers and a baguette in the basket.

They can be heavy, slow and fairly basic in their functionality, but they look so beautiful that it's hard to mind. Once upon a time, shoppers came in black or cream, but now manufacturers are vastly widening the colour palette of these bikes.

Pros
Just look at them! These gorgeous machines sum up the stylish, slightly vintage aesthetic of cycling perfectly. Their low, curved bars and lack of speed credentials mean they are ideal for those who enjoy breezing along in floaty dresses rather than pounding the roads in Lycra.

Cons
Heavy, fairly basic, not suitable for off-roading or excessively rough terrain.

 What I ride

'I have a ladies' shopper and I love it to pieces. The crossbar is very low so I can just hop on and off it, even in a skirt, without exposing myself to any unfortunate passers-by. I like to go fast, so the poor brakes are always taking a hammering and I suppose technically speaking my bike isn't built for the kind of hard use I subject it to, but it always gets me where I want to go in style.' - Janie, 26

Single-speed and fixed-wheel bikes

Single-speed and fixed-wheel models are bikes stripped down to the very basics. Two wheels, two pedals and a frame – and that's about it. These bikes have a narrow frame with flat or dropped handlebars and come in a range of eye-catching colours. They are ripe for customizing, accessorizing and being made truly unique. They are popular where a lack of real hills makes riding through town with only one gear entirely feasible, and are beloved of hipsters the world over. Single-speed bikes come with a rear brake, whereas most fixed-wheel bikes do not. On fixed-wheel bikes, there is no freewheel mechanism, so the bike will only move if the pedals are moving. Braking is achieved by slowing or stopping pedalling. Again, I can't think of a car analogy, as most have gears and brakes.

Pros
These bikes are totally blank canvases and can be customized in any way. Cycling at its most stripped down, skilful and pure. Uber trendy among the hipster movement.

Cons
Little luxuries like gears and brakes were probably invented for a reason. Not ideal for hilly or off-road terrain.

Electric bikes

These bikes are growing in popularity. They combine the traditional pedalling mechanism with a small electric motor, so are best compared to pedal-powered mopeds or scooters. This saves your energy and means you can cycle longer, further and quicker but still get a workout. They tend to be more expensive at entry level than an ordinary bicycle, but if you have a particularly long commute to work and still want to cycle, an electric bike can nevertheless save you money. They are also ridiculously good fun.

Pros
Quicker and easier than a standard bike, ideal for longer journeys, brilliant fun.

Cons
Less of a workout than an ordinary bike unless you cover dramatically longer distances, more expensive.

Choosing the right bike for you

Your bike has to fit in with your lifestyle and environment as well as your budget and personal tastes. A sleek, twitchy road bike won't do well on muddy country tracks, and a big mountain bike might be a squeeze in a tiny city apartment. Here are some points to consider before you choose your bike:

Where do you live?

Countryside
Hills, off-road tracks and paths just beg to be explored by bike. A mountain bike or a more robust hybrid will make the most of uneven terrain, slopes and woodland tracks. A shopper or a touring bike will withstand the odd bump and glide easily down country lanes.

Suburbs/town
Any type of bike will adapt to a suburban environment well. Go for a mountain bike if you want to take it out into the sticks, or a road, touring or fixed-wheel bike for more urban expeditions. A shopper is perfect for pottering through town, and a folding bike is ideal for commuting from the suburbs into the big city. A hybrid is also ideally suited to the suburban commuter. If you have quite a distance to travel to work, an electric bike will fit the bill.

City
The fixed-wheel bike comes into its own in cities, as does the shopper. Hybrids once again are perfect for urban biking, and road and touring bikes will get you round speedily and in style. There's nothing stopping you using a mountain bike in the city – I did for years – but you won't be the fastest cyclist on the road. Folding bikes are perfect for city life, as you can take them with you on public transport and tuck them away in the office, a bar or at home.

How much space do you have?

Loads
The bike world is your oyster! If you have a garage, shed or basement big enough for a bike, then any type will suit.

A bit
Smaller-framed road or fixed-wheel bikes take up less space than chunkier mountain bikes or shoppers. But as long as you have a spare room, a small garden or yard or even a hallway, you should be able to store most types of bike easily enough. If you live in an apartment block or a flat on the first or second floor, make sure your bike is light enough to be easily carried up stairs, or will fit into a lift/elevator. Or look at the reception area to see if there is anywhere you can leave your bike – safely locked up, of course.

Not much/none at all
A folding bike will pack up nice and small and squeeze into the tiniest of cupboards. Alternatively, innovative storage solutions such as wall-mounted hangings or racks will turn your bike into the ultimate in interior décor. Smaller, lighter-framed bikes such as road, touring or fixed-wheel models will hang better than a clumpy mountain bike or heavy shopper.

What I ride
'I have a road bike, which I chose because it was decent, relatively lightweight, suitable for longer cycle rides – and it was within my budget. I love it, although I do get bike envy at traffic lights.' – Lou, 32

The next step is to look at your budget

Firstly, find out if your workplace does any kind of cycle loan or cycle-to-work scheme. These range from simple loans – where your employer provides the lump sum for you to buy your bike and equipment, and you pay the total back over a set period – to government-funded schemes that can save you hundreds on the cost of a bike. Your HR department or co-ordinator will be able to tell you if there is a scheme in place where you are based.

If your workplace does not have a cycle-to-work or bike loan scheme in place, why not suggest they look into it as an additional employee benefit with excellent environmental credentials?

Realistically, you are going to need a small lump sum to kit yourself out with a very basic bike, helmet, lights and a lock, which are the bare essentials. £500/$800 is a good sum to set aside, as this will allow you to buy a decent bike and other accessories such as bags, panniers, a rack and a jacket. Remember, if you use your bike in place of a car, train or bus, you will automatically be saving money. After the initial outlay, maintaining a bike is very cheap. Think how much you currently spend on petrol or train tickets – even better, actually add up how much travelling costs you every year. Using your bike in place of a car or train just once a week will amount to a considerable saving over a year. If you use your bike as your primary form of transport, you can save yourself hundreds or even thousands.

Bike
The majority of your budget should go on the bike itself. If you buy new, you will need a minimum of around £200/$320 for an entry-level hybrid, fixed-wheel, shopper or mountain bike. These more basic models will still do a fantastic job of getting you from A to B. Splash out more if you want a lighter, better put-together, prettier bike or one with more up-to-date technology. The

price point for a road, electric, touring or folding bike at entry level is much higher, as these are more specialist types of bike.

If money is tight, go second hand. Look on eBay for bargains or try online classified sites. Put up an advert at your workplace or in your local shop detailing what you're looking for. Or dig out that old bike you used to ride when you were a teenager. Chances are it's still usable, so take it to a shop to have some new brake pads fitted and generally give it a bit of TLC. If you never had a bike when you were younger, ask friends and family members if any of them have an old bike rotting away in the garage or garden shed they'd be happy for you to take off their hands. Or investigate bike loan schemes in your area.

Lock
Buy the best lock you can afford. You really do get what you pay for with locks, with the more expensive types offering the most security. Some of the very heavy-duty locks come with their own guarantee and insurance. D-locks are very popular because they are secure and compact and can be attached to the frame of many bikes while they are in use. You can also buy heavier chains, coated in textile or plastic. It would take a very determined thief to saw through one of these, and most can be easily carried in a rucksack, over your shoulder or around your waist. Again, if money is tight, go second hand. Most locks are built to last, and last, and last!

Lights
It is a legal requirement for bikes in the UK used between sundown and sunrise to be fitted with lights. In the US, the law varies by state, but making yourself as visible as possible simply makes sense. At the very least you must have a white front and red rear light fitted. A halogen lamp fitted to your front handlebars will aid your own visibility. You must also have reflectors and most, if not all, new bikes will come with these fitted as standard.

Above: Who said helmets didn't look good?

As a general rule, when it comes to lights, the more the merrier. Trussing your bike up like a Christmas tree will only stand in your favour. And don't stop at your bike. If you wear a helmet, fit a light to the back of it, and put a light on your bag, too.

Bike insurance

Unfortunately, bikes are prime pinching material and, despite everyone's best efforts, bike theft continues to be a problem especially in urban areas. Bike insurance is an affordable way of knowing you can replace your bike should it be spirited away, and some policies may also insure you for personal injury or for any damage that you may cause. Insurance companies may stipulate that you must use a certain lock in order for the insurance to be valid. In some cases, your bike may be covered by your home or contents insurance – check before simply assuming you are covered.

Helmet

If there are laws requiring you to wear a cycling helmet, as in some states in the US for under-16s, then ensure you comply with that law at all times. However, for most adults in the UK and the US, legally there is no obligation to wear a helmet.

Your helmet needs to fit properly, so take advice from the sales assistant or, if you are buying online, check the measurements and dimensions carefully. A badly-fitting helmet is utterly pointless! Make sure your helmet meets up-to-date safety standards. For the UK, this is currently BS EN 1078: 1997. For the US, there are several standards – the CPSC's standards and the Snell standards, which can exceed the CPSC's. The B-90 is similar to the CPSC's, and the B-95 is a more rigorous test. Snell regularly audits helmets on the market, ensuring they meet safety standards.

The helmet argument

There is a lively, ongoing debate surrounding bicycle helmets. Some feel strongly that wearing a helmet should be made a legal requirement. Others, myself included, feel it is a personal choice but also simply common sense to wear one. Helmets seem to be to cyclists what speed cameras are to motorists – a divisive topic. Here are some of the arguments for and against so that you can make up your own mind.

Arguments for wearing a cycle helmet
Common sense tells us that having some protection between our precious skulls and the road is bound to be beneficial should we happen to find ourselves hurtling head first towards that road.

A 2009 study by the independent UK transport organization Transport Research Laboratory found that cycle helmets can help prevent head and brain injuries, particularly if no other vehicle is involved. TRL also found that 40 per cent of cyclists admitted to hospital following a collision had head injuries. A study carried out in Seattle in 1989 concluded that helmets could prevent 85 per cent of head injuries and 88 per cent of brain injuries. A second study, carried out in 1987, found that cycle helmets could prevent up to 90 per cent of fatalities.

Anecdotally, almost everybody in cycling circles knows somebody whose helmet 'saved their life', although clearly there is no scientific evidence for these claims.

Arguments against wearing a cycling helmet
The studies that gave rise to the impressive statistics about cycle helmets preventing head injuries, brain injuries and fatalities are out of date and have simply not been proved in real life. There has been no real reduction in head injuries or fatalities in countries where cyclists are required by law to wear a helmet.

Cyclists may be inclined to behave more recklessly if they are wearing a helmet, as they assume they are protected, and by turn, motorists may be less likely to drive carefully around them for the same reason. I have also heard it argued more than once that instead of focusing on forcing cyclists to wear helmets, there should be a better infrastructure for cyclists with safer cycle lanes and more consideration from motorists.

Cycle helmets are not the equivalent of motorcycle crash helmets and opponents of helmet enforcement argue that bike helmets are far less safe and offer far less protection than the pro-helmet lobby claims.

Conclusions
Wading through all that, we can draw two main conclusions. Firstly, a cycle helmet is not guaranteed to save your life or protect you from head injury should you be involved in a nasty accident. But secondly, it might.

A degree of common sense is required. Helmets are not a substitute for safe cycling. I do believe it is more important to cycle safely than it is to wear a helmet. But if you cycle safely and wear a helmet, you have the best of both worlds, with an understanding that accidents do happen and nothing in life is ever 100 per cent risk free.

Helmets may give you the confidence to cycle assertively, which is essential if you are to remain safe. Your personal safety is your own responsibility, as well as the responsibility of others, so to not wear a helmet because you think it's entirely down to motorists to ensure your safety seems rather akin to cutting your nose off to spite your face.

Wherever you stand on the helmet debate, it is better to own one than not, so you always have the option of wearing it available to you.

In the shop

There are several 'bike supermarket' chains that will stock pretty much everything you need, but independent bike shops are also a good bet for quality, impartial advice and more niche bikes and accessories.

When choosing your bike, take your time and try out several different sizes and models to be entirely sure you are getting exactly what you want. Don't feel pressured to make a decision immediately. You wouldn't necessarily buy the first pair of jeans you try on, and it's no different with bikes. Take your time and shop around until you find something that fits you perfectly.

Women's specific design bikes versus men's bikes

As men and women are anatomically different, women's specific design (WSD) bikes are a different shape to men's. Typically, the crossbar is lower and the bikes are shorter. Some women find WSD bikes more comfortable and easier to ride, and they tend to come in more feminine colour schemes. However, many women also choose to ride men's bikes, as the selection of WSD bikes, particularly beyond entry level, can be fairly limited. Manufacturers are responding to the increased demand from women, but there is still more choice among male-specific models. When choosing your bike, try out both men's and WSD bikes, and if you prefer the fit and feel of a man's bike, then go ahead and choose one.

Most cycle shop assistants will be helpful and supportive. They are there to offer you advice as well as sell you a bike, so use their expertise and ask questions about the bikes you are trying out. Tell them what you plan to use the bike for and use their advice to help you make a decision. But never feel pressurized into straying away from what you want. If the shop assistant is trying to sell you a soulless black hybrid and you've got

your heart set on a pink shopper, stick to your guns and tell them. Most bikes are well built enough to withstand regular use. Likewise, if the assistant is trying to steer you towards ladylike shoppers but you want a sporty mountain bike or a sleek touring bike, tell them so and don't let them pigeonhole you.

When you leave the shop, you should feel happy and excited about your bike. The principles of shopping are universal – take your time trying things on until you find something that fits perfectly and makes you look fantastic.

Your new bike might need adjusting to fit you perfectly. Later on in the book we will look at adjusting the handlebars and saddle yourself, but when buying your bike, ask the assistant to set it up for you there in the store. They will also be able to show you exactly how to change the height of the handlebars and saddle. Ask what size of inner tube your bike needs and the type of valve, so that you know what to ask for when you're stocking up on spares.

Buying second hand

Second-hand bikes are perfect for budget-conscious cyclistas. But even if you know you are going to buy second hand, visit a bike shop first to try out new bikes and pick the brains of the sales assistants. This will help you establish what size and type of bike you need.

Some bike stores, particularly independent shops, will sell second-hand bikes. Most of these will have been serviced before going on sale and may even come with a warranty to give you added peace of mind.

It is often cheaper, however, to buy online, through sites like eBay, through classified adverts or from friends of friends. In this case, the most important thing to establish is that the bike they are selling is not stolen.

Ask questions about the bike. When did the seller buy it? Where from? How regularly has it been used? Why are they selling it? Do they have the logbook or service record that came with the bike when they bought it new? Do they still have the receipt? Trust your instincts and if something sounds dodgy or appears too good to be true, then it probably is. There is no real way to establish for sure that the seller is legitimate, but use your judgement. If in doubt, don't buy.

The condition of the bike largely depends on how much you are willing to pay. The less you pay, the less you get. Worn brake pads, tyres or wires and a rusty chain can easily be replaced. Scratched or damaged paintwork is a purely aesthetic problem. Rust or large cracks on the frame, the gears or the cogs or damaged wheels are more severe problems and best avoided.

Take the bike for a test ride if it is being sold in a roadworthy condition. Check that you are happy and comfortable on it and that there are no ominous clicking noises, creaks, groans or slipping gears. If the bike is not roadworthy in its current condition, at least hop on it to check the size is suitable. Saddles and handlebars can be adjusted, but if you're stretching to get over the crossbar or to reach the handlebars at all, then the bike is too big. If you feel uncomfortably cramped, the bike is too small.

If possible, take a friend with you to give you a second opinion.

Don't allow yourself to be pressured into making an instant decision or paying more than you can afford or feel the bike is worth. If the seller starts giving you the hard sell, walk away. There are plenty of second-hand bikes out there, you don't have to buy the first one you see.

Take your second-hand bargain into a cycle shop for a quick once-over and service to get it fully back up to roadworthy standards.

Now that you are fully kitted out, it's time to get on that bike!

What I ride
'I have a second-hand Raleigh, which I chose mainly because it was cheap and comfortable. I love it and I feel in an odd sort of way that we've been through a lot together, so I feel like it has a sort of personality.' – Laura, 33

Right: If you're on a budget, look into buying a second-hand or 'preloved' bike.

3

getting started

You've chosen and bought your perfect bike and it's sat gleaming in front of you. Congratulations! You have taken an important step towards becoming a fully-fledged cyclista.

The next step is to get on that thing and get moving. Don't become one of those would-be cyclists whose bikes sit around gathering dust while they find excuse after excuse about why they aren't cycling.

Total beginners

If you have never been on a bike in your life, then you will need some help to get started. It does take a little while to get your balance and learn the basics. The best way is to sign up for some cycling lessons.

A quick internet search should help you find a professionally accredited cycling instructor in your local area. A qualified instructor will be able to help you learn the ropes, provide encouragement and ensure you are fully versed in essential road safety before you hit the streets.

You will need to find a quiet spot in which to practise, well away from any traffic. Parks are good, and grass is a softer landing should you struggle at first. Business parks and industrial estates are usually completely empty after working hours and on Saturdays and Sundays, and will

Left: The saying 'it's like riding a bike' exists for a reason. Practise until you are confident enough to hit the roads.

provide blissful respite from the general public. Wear old, comfortable clothing and a helmet. Try and practise by yourself in between cycling lessons, following the processes your instructor showed you. But don't be tempted to hit the open road alone until you have practised alongside your instructor and are confident that you can manage traffic.

Getting back into the swing

If you rode a bike when you were a child, as most of us did, the ability to ride a bike will not have left you. Even if it has been years since you looked at anything with two wheels, the innate ability to balance and control a bike will have stuck. Remind yourself of this before you get on and keep reminding yourself, however nervous you feel, that you do know how to do this. Trust your instincts. Picture yourself cycling confidently and happily. It will not take long for that image to become a reality.

To start off, find a quiet spot where you can practise without interuption or risk. As above, consider parks or deserted business parks. Choose somewhere with as little passing traffic as possible.

Take it slowly at first. Get used to the feel of the bike and familiarize yourself with your brakes. If your bike is brand new, the brakes will be exceptionally sharp, so be gentle with them and take your time getting to know how much pressure you need to apply. Practise setting off, changing up and down the gears, if you have them, slowing down and stopping. Next, start to turn gently left and right. Work on easy curves at first and build up until you are able to ride your bike in a complete circle. Then start turning sharply left and right. This will enable you to turn corners on your bike.

On pages 46–48 there are a few exercises to help you practise the basics and get used to being on a bike again.

Some useful exercises

These little drills will help you get used to handling your bike and performing basic manoeuvres. Enlist a friend and head to a park or other open space to practise before heading out onto the roads.

1 High five!

This exercise will help you get used to taking a hand off the handlebars, to signal left or right.

Get a friend to come out with you and stand in the middle of the path or park. As you cycle past them, take the hand nearest to them off the handlebars and give them a high five. Return your hand to the handlebars, turn around and practise on the other side.

2 Emergency stops

These are absolutely essential. You never know when you may have to brake sharply, so it is vital that you know how your bike will react when you slam on the brakes. You also need to understand the impact upon your bike if you use the front brake only, the rear brake only or both brakes together. The front brake will stop the front wheel, the back brake the back wheel. As a rule, you want to lead from the rear wheel, so apply the rear brake first or, if you need to stop immediately, both brakes together. If you apply the front brake only with any force, you may find yourself flying gracefully over the handlebars and landing on your derriere. If you apply the rear brake only with force, chances are you will skid.

Practise braking using the rear brake, the front brake and both brakes until you are able to slow down and stop in the shortest time possible.

3 How many?

You will need to be able to look behind you to check there is no-one trying to overtake you as you turn left or right or change lanes. Practise this in a safe spot. Get a friend to stand behind you and hold up one or both hands – glance back and tell them how many fingers they are holding up. Practise this looking back over both your left and right shoulders.

When translating this exercise to the road, you need to spend as little time as possible looking behind you. We are talking a cursory glance to ensure you are not pulling out into anybody's path. If you spend too much time looking behind you, you might not notice what's happening in front of you.

4 Figure of eight

Balance is crucial and it can be hard to avoid wobbling when you turn left or right at first. Practise cycling in figures of eight – if possible, get a friend to lay out a course for you using traffic cones or other markers.

Take it slowly at first as you weave in and out, then pick up speed as you become more balanced.

5 Up you get!

Standing up to pedal can give you more speed and momentum – and get you up those pesky hills.

Practise standing up on your pedals, then sitting gracefully back down. Once you are comfortable with this, practise pedalling while standing up. Feel how much more power you can generate – and feel the burn in your thighs and bottom!

6 Signalling

When cycling on roads, you will need to signal, just as vehicles indicate, to let other road users know of your intentions and avoid a collision.

Signalling on your bike could not be easier. If you are turning left, take your left hand off the handlebars and extend your left arm. If you are turning right, do the same with the right arm. That's all there is to it! Always remember to take a quick glance behind you before signalling and turning, to check you are not pulling out into the path of oncoming traffic.

Road sense and safety

If you drive, you will be familiar with the rules of the road. But roads are very different places from the cushioned inside of a car. A good driver does not automatically translate into a good cyclist.

If you don't drive, your road sense and knowledge may be very limited. Other than understanding that a red light means stop and a green light means go, you may not have any idea of what traffic signals mean and of the safest way to behave on the roads.

In the UK, the Highway Code outlines the rules of the road and best practice when it comes to road safety. There is no US equivalent of the Highway Code, but advice is available from the Department for Transportation. Road safety organizations and charities in the US and the UK also offer a wealth of advice and information, usually free of charge.

Cyclists are fully entitled to use the roads and do not have to stick to cycle lanes. You can also cycle on designated off-road cycle paths. You must not, however, cycle on pavements/sidewalks and in the UK and some parts of the US it is actually against the law. Don't be tempted to 'work yourself up to it' by cycling on pavements/sidewalks before hitting the roads. Practise in parks instead. If you feel uncomfortable on the road at any time, get off and push your bike along the pavement.

The best way to learn vital and often life-saving road safety and sense is to take lessons with a professional cycling instructor or on an approved cycling and road safety course. Some courses run by local authorities or organizations are even available free of charge. A book or set of guidelines can only teach you so much and there is no substitute for practical, tailored experience in a live setting from a qualified professional. There is a directory of contacts at the back of this book.

Getting used to life on two wheels

Don't attempt the open road alone for the first time. Go out with an instructor or ask a friend, colleague or partner who cycles to come out with you a few times. Plan the route you will take and agree how you will let them know if you want to stop. Shouting 'stop' is always a good one.

Your friend or instructor should cycle either ahead of you or next to you. Follow their lead and watch how they interact with traffic. If your friend is cycling too fast, let them know and don't be afraid to pull over and stop if you need to.

If you don't have a friend who cycles, contact a local cycling club or network, or ask around at your workplace to see if there are any cyclists who can help you. Most cyclists love their hobby and will be delighted to help out a beginner.

Positioning

Position yourself a comfortable distance away from the kerb. The ideal distance is about 1 metre/3 feet. This will ensure motorists can see you and will help you avoid a nasty collision with a car door should one suddenly open into your path.

Interacting with motorists

Motorists will pass you as and when they are able, and most should be kind enough to give you a wide berth. If they have to follow you for a distance because there are no overtaking opportunities and you start to feel uncomfortable, you can pull in and let them overtake you. Most motorists are decent human beings and will not mind following a cyclist for a short distance until

Left: Cycling with an experienced friend will help you build up your confidence and ability.

it is safe to overtake. However, you do not have to give way to motorists or pull over for them – you are as entitled to use the road as they are.

A very small yet loathsome minority may rev their engines, flash their lights, toot their horns and shout at you to get out of the way. Never risk life and limb engaging or arguing with such an idiot. Ignore them and proceed as if they were not there. If you are genuinely frightened, pull over and let them go on ahead and be unpleasant somewhere else. It is never worth risking your own safety to prove a point.

When cycling in company, cycle in single file wherever possible on busy roads or at peak times. Do not cycle more than two abreast. Respect other road users if you want them to respect you. Holding up traffic so that you can have a nice chat isn't very respectful to others.

Finally, do not assume motorists can see you – make sure they can see you, every step of the way. Make eye contact with motorists. Rap on car bonnets/hoods or windows if you have to, if somebody is getting a bit too close. You must be seen at all times. I cannot stress this enough. Repeat after me. You must be seen. You must be seen. YOU MUST BE SEEN.

Roundabouts and junctions

Try to avoid roundabouts and busy junctions until you are sure you can manage them. Again, this is where cycling with someone else is invaluable, as they will be able to guide you until you are confident enough to attempt it yourself. A cycling instructor can also help you learn to cope with roundabouts, junctions and busy roads.

Until you are completely confident negotiating roundabouts and junctions, get off your bike at a safe spot and push it across the road at a pedestrian crossing or push it along the pavement/sidewalk next to the roundabout.

Cycle lanes

The cycling community is not always universally in favour of cycle lanes. Many large cities have sophisticated networks of lanes and things are improving all the time, but many cycle lanes remain inadequate at best. Internet memes exist of particularly impractical or ridiculous cycle lanes, including those with large obstacles such as trees or dustbins/trash cans slap bang in the middle, and those which terminate abruptly for no apparent reason.

Some cycle lanes can be positively dangerous, such as those that take you up the inside of heavy traffic approaching a busy junction or those that are extremely narrow, forcing you to hug the gutter as traffic storms past a hair's breadth from your handlebars.

Therefore always remember that you do not have to use, or stick to, cycle lanes. They are there if you need them, and they can be useful, but they are entirely optional. Remain 1 metre/3 feet from the kerb wherever possible. If there is a cycle lane narrower than this, do not use the cycle lane. You have the right – and the freedom – to use the entire carriageway.

A word on gender stereotypes

I have read more than one report alleging that women are more likely to adopt an apologetic, 'don't mind me, I'm not really here' style of cycling. I'm talking hugging kerbs, sticking religiously to cycle lanes, trying to assist oncoming traffic by 'helpfully' waving cars past instead of looking where you are going, that kind of thing. Whereas men are more likely to assert their rights and cycle confidently to the point of aggression, sometimes downright antagonizing motorists in the name of 'educating' them.

This assertion is pretty sexist, but there is a certain type of cyclist – who can be male or female – who prioritizes manners over safety. And there is a

Above: Cycling lanes are a useful option but remember you do not have to stick to them at all costs. You have as much right to use the road as any motorist.

certain type of cyclist who prioritizes rights and proving a point over safety. I have heard many, and I admit usually female, cyclists talking about wanting to be polite and considerate to other road users and follow the rules. 'I can't overtake traffic on the outside, I'll get beeped at!' 'I have to stick to cycle lanes because that's what the Highway Code recommends.' 'I can't position myself in the middle of the carriageway, I'd feel so self-conscious holding up traffic.' I have also heard many, this time usually male, cyclists talking about asserting their rights on the road. 'Why should I pull over for a motorist? They can wait.' 'If somebody is aggressive, I'm going to hold them up for as long as possible to teach them a lesson.' 'If I have right of way, I'm going whether there's oncoming traffic or not. Motorists need to learn to give way to cyclists.' Don't be one of those cyclists.

Let me break this down for you. Being beeped at never killed anybody. Feeling self-conscious never killed anybody. Failing to follow recommendations to the letter in favour of using common sense in certain situations never killed anybody. Conceding right of way never killed anybody. Not being seen by motorists and taking excessive risks sadly does kill people. Accidents do happen, but many incidents are preventable.

If you are going to use the roads, you need to be confident. You absolutely cannot allow car horns, or the occasional comment from a particularly irritable motorist, to compromise your safety. You cannot make the comfort and ease of other motorists your priority. Leave the manners at home where they belong and look after number one. Your safety is your own responsibility and you cannot rely on the goodwill of other road users – you must look after yourself.

But you also need to remember that as a cyclist you are vulnerable. Your duty is to keep yourself safe, not 'educate' motorists or act as a conduit for cyclist–motorist relations. You don't need to be a role model. You don't need to become a one-woman crusade for cyclist's rights. You do need to stay safe at all times, at all costs. And, as always – *you must be seen*.

Building confidence

Often the most difficult thing is getting the confidence to start in the first place. If you've had visions of yourself zipping along on a neat little shopper with a basket full of flowers and French bread on a sunny Saturday morning, and in reality you are wobbling about like mad and struggling

to master turning left and right in the hammering rain, it's easy to get discouraged. Stick at it. You will get better and you are capable of becoming an accomplished cyclist. The only way to get better, is to practice. If you find yourself losing motivation, ask yourself why...

Are you genuinely struggling to master cycling? Take lessons with a qualified cycling instructor. Are you a bit disillusioned and fed up of pottering around the block but not confident enough to hit the roads for real? Have a couple of lessons with an instructor to boost your confidence. Ask a friend to come out cycling with you, or send an email around the office asking for a cycling buddy. Contact a cycling club or network, or put a request up on a cycling forum.

Are you feeling unfit and knackered after a sedate five-minute journey or struggling to keep up with friends on their bikes? Take comfort in the knowledge that if you can manage a five-minute journey today, then next week you'll be fit enough to cycle for ten minutes. Cycling is ideal for building fitness, as if you are really out of breath, you can slow right down or even stop, catch your breath, then start pushing on again.

Busting those excuses

As a newbie cyclist, you might find yourself making the occasional excuse to leave your bike at home and take the train, especially if your confidence is low. Perhaps the weather is a bit grim, or you've taken a tumble and suffered a few bruises – particularly to your ego. If you're desperate for a day off, then go for it – but don't talk yourself into quitting. Here's how to keep yourself in the saddle.

1 'But it's raining!'

A bit of rain never hurt anybody. Put on a waterproof jacket, cover your hair, grit your teeth and give it a go. Take care, as road surfaces may be slippery in the wet. Visibility is also reduced in the rain, so switch your lights on and wear high-visibility outerwear, even if it's the middle of the day. Allow extra time for braking. Enjoy the freedom.

2 '*I fell off and hurt myself and now I don't want to get back on*'

Ouch! Poor you. Falling off is rare, but it happens, and it's not nice. Fortunately, it doesn't happen very often. Chances are you will have a graze or bruise here and there, so patch yourself up and have a cup of tea, then get back on. The longer you leave it, the more intimidating the thought of getting back on will become. Have a session with a cycling instructor to restore your confidence.

3 '*I don't think I'm the right build for cycling*'

There is no such thing as 'the right build'. Anybody can cycle. Cyclists come in all shapes and sizes, and regular cycling will tone and improve your figure considerably.

4 '*My bum hurts!*'

If you haven't cycled in a long time, then the first few sessions will be hard on your posterior. Your body will quickly get used to spending time on a saddle, but until then, a gel saddle cover or padded cycling shorts will give a bit of extra cushioning. Whenever you begin a new workout regime, your body will hurt in strange places, but you will adapt.

5 '*There's nowhere to store my bike.*'

There are plenty of places if you look hard enough. Look out for solid and immobile objects that your lock can fit around, such as lamp posts, bike racks or street signs. Be careful of anything that a lock could potentially be lifted over or under. Remove and take with you anything that can be easily taken off your bike, such as lights or a bag. Some cyclists like to remove the saddle or a wheel from their bike, to further deter thieves. Bike insurance and a high-quality lock will give you peace of mind about leaving your pride and joy locked up in public.

6 '*It's so hilly where I live*'

There are few hills that can't be conquered in a very low gear – and what goes up must come down, so once you've slugged your way to the top, you get a nice easy freewheel all the way back down again. Hill cycling is fabulous for fitness and it works the upper body too.

7 '*I'm so busy. I just can't find the time*'

You know that saying: 'If you want something done, ask a busy person'? Genuinely busy people know how to prioritize and manage their time. Be honest with yourself. Are you really as busy as you tell everybody you are? Or are you just busy telling everybody that you're busy? Genuinely busy people don't sit around talking about how busy they are – they get on with it.

Genuinely busy people don't 'find' the time – they make time. They get up an hour earlier or sacrifice an hour of mindless TV. What about that hour you spent over lunch browsing Facebook, the two hours in front of the TV at night, the lie-in until 10 am at the weekend? That's all time you could have spent cycling.

8 '*It's a bit cold and dark for cycling at the moment, I'll wait until the weather improves before I start*'

Don't be such a wimp. Wrap up warm and light your bike up like a Christmas tree. Just a short cycle will raise your heart rate and warm you up, burn calories and help justify a hot chocolate at the end of your journey.

Motivation 101

Muireann Carey-Campbell, aka fashion and fitness blogger Bangs and a Bun

Muireann Carey-Campbell, aka fashion and fitness blogger Bangs and a Bun, is known the Internet over for her first-class motivational skills. Her website, www.spikesandheels.com, embraces fitness for women who want to feel great for life, not just shed a few pounds in time for Christmas.

Here, she shares her thoughts on staying motivated for an active lifestyle. If you still find yourself flagging, and frequently opting for the car over cycling, then this little pep talk is bound to get you off your backside and onto your bike.

'My whole thing with fitness is that it's a lifestyle. It's not this separate thing that's compartmentalized into one hour a week in the gym or saved for a day I've eaten too much cake – it's who I am. I'm a runner. The more I run, the more I love other types of training.' A bike was inevitable, and after much shopping around I found "the one" – a white Dolan fixed-wheel track bike with drop handles. It is supremely badass.

'The bike now allows me to take that a step further. It's both a way to commute and a way to work on my core and leg strength. Meetings I can't run to, I can bike to and not miss out on my fitness fix. Birds, stones and all of that.

'Working out, be it running, cycling or boxing, makes me feel fantastic. It clears my head and makes me happy. Part of the reason I started my site Spikes and Heels was out of frustration. Most fitness media aimed at women is pink, fluffy and all about weight loss, as if there's no other benefit to exercise. It's such a dangerous message, casting working out almost as a punishment.

'And of course, exercise aimed at women is all Bums 'n' Tums and Zumba, which is all fine, but what about those of us who want to push harder, do more? Contrary to popular belief, it is actually OK for women to sweat. You can be pretty on rest days. So passionate am I about this that 'Be Pretty on Rest Days' is actually the tag line of the Spikes and Heels website. If what our hair and make-up look like is taking priority over our health and fitness, we've gotten a little mixed up along the way somewhere.

'So I say, grab a bike, embrace the helmet hair, race that taxi to the traffic light, grunt as you power up that hill and wear the dust you picked up riding a dirt track with pride. Ultimately, striving to be the best you can be, in mind, body and soul, is the epitome of beauty and femininity.'

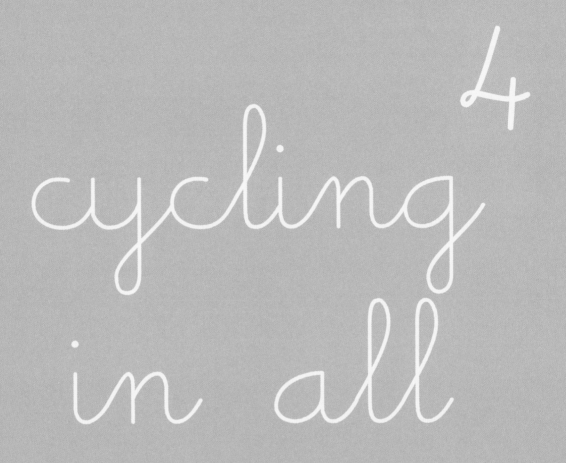

cycling in all seasons

4

This page: However you get to work, chances are you can cycle at least some of the way. Folding bikes are brilliant for urban commuters.

Now you're a fully-fledged cycling superstar, bursting with motivation and a can-do attitude, it's time to look at incorporating cycling into your daily life.

The first step is to think about how you travel every day and how you can switch to making the journey by bike. The most obvious and practical solution is to cycle to work, so we'll start there.

Cycling to work

Could you? Should you? Probably, and yes! Unless your commute to work involves an aeroplane, it's likely that you can incorporate cycling into at least some of your journey. We'll talk about the practicalities of arriving at work post-cycle and getting yourself glammed up ready for the day ahead in Chapter Five, Looking Good While Cycling. Firstly, let's consider how feasible it is for you to cycle in the first place, by looking at how you currently get into work.

Walking

Simple! Just hop on your bike instead. You'll save heaps of time, so why not use that time to take a longer route to work? It will give you more of a workout and set you up nicely for the day ahead.

Driving

Again, just swap the car for the bike. A commute of less than 10 km/6 miles shouldn't take longer than an hour, which is a reasonable length of time to spend travelling to work. Once you've worked on your fitness and picked up a bit of speed, you'll probably be able to manage it in half that time. If your journey is longer than this, you could tackle the entire journey by bike, or break it up. I have

met people who have commuted up to 48 km/30 miles by bike on a daily basis and thought nothing of it. In fact, I have been one of those people and can honestly say I've never been fitter and more toned in my life.

But plenty of cyclists split the journey, by finding a parking spot halfway between home and work and cycling part of the way, then driving the rest (or the other way round). Just pop the bike in the back of your car or lock it up somewhere safe. Swap the car for a bike–train or bike–underground combination if that's more feasible. Or look into an electric bike instead.

Tackle motorways or speedy highways during your commute? Look for an alternative route, consider swapping to a bike–train combination of travel or drive the high-speed section, then park up and cycle the rest of the way.

Public transport

As with driving, just swap the train, underground/subway, bus, tram or shuttle for your bike! If your journey is too long for you to comfortably cycle the entire way, find a good halfway point and cycle half the journey, leave your bike safely locked up, then use public transport for the rest. Public bike hire schemes, such as Barclays Bikes in London, Vélib' in Paris or Citi Bike in New York, are ideal for this kind of journey, too. Or opt for a folding bike that you can take on the train or tube/subway with you.

Persuaded to give cycling to work a go? Great! Here are a few steps you can take to prepare yourself and ensure all goes smoothly:

Familiarize yourself
Practise cycling the route to and from work before you do it for real. Even if you've walked, or driven the route a thousand times before, I promise you it will look and feel different from a bicycle.

Time the route
Be aware it will be a different prospect during rush hour, when there are likely to be more cyclists, motorists and pedestrians out on the roads. So allow plenty of extra time on top.

Why I cycle

'I started cycling to avoid the stress and expense of public transport. I commute to work every day and also spend a day each weekend exploring new areas. Cycling has become a positive part of my daily life and I feel guilty if I forget it. Cycling is currently ridiculously en mode for trendies – proper road riding with all the gear is still not considered 'cool', but personally I prefer to feel more functional than fashionable when I ride.' **- Jules, 26**

Be prepared
Pack a pump, spare inner tube and spare batteries for your lights into your bag and keep them there at all times. The minute you use up your spares, cycle to the nearest supplier and replace them immediately. You do not want to be faced with a puncture, no spare inner tube and a long walk into work when your boss is expecting a presentation at 9 am!

Buddy up
Unless you are perfectly confident, find a buddy to cycle with at first. You can pace – and encourage – each other, and they will know the route inside out. Put an advert on your work intranet or put the word out among your network that you're hoping to start cycling in and looking to buddy up. If nobody else at your workplace cycles, try offices and workplaces nearby, a local cycling club or an online cycling forum. Experienced cyclists are usually happy to help beginners.

Have a session with a cycling instructor
Do this beforehand to sharpen up your road sense and skills. If possible, get them to cycle the route to work with you.

Fixing punctures
Practise fixing punctures and putting your chain back on, so that you know what to do in the event of any problems. See Chapter Six, Keeping Your Bike Healthy, for advice on basic maintenance.

Mechanical problems
Have the number of your nearest bike shop or cycling workshop saved in your mobile/cell phone in the event of any mechanical problems you can't deal with yourself.

Allow yourself loads of time
Not only for the cycle itself, but you will need time to get yourself prepared before you leave and transformed from bike chic to office goddess once you arrive. See Chapter Five, Looking Good While Cycling, for more advice.

Cycling for fitness

We all know that regular exercise is incredibly good for us both physically and mentally. Exercise helps you focus, de-stress and relax as well as doing wonderful things for your body and your overall health.

The benefits of cycling as exercise are multiple. It is truly inclusive and there are few people who genuinely cannot cycle. It is a low-impact activity, meaning it is easier on your joints than running or 'feel the burn'-style workout classes. But it can still burn up in excess of 500 calories an hour, as well as toning legs, thighs and the upper body if you add hills to the mix.

For solitary types who enjoy their own company, getting out and about on a bike is extremely cathartic and offers much-needed 'me time'. For social butterflies who love company and meeting new people, cycling is a great way to make new friends and bond through a shared interest and experience. In short, there's something in it for everybody, which makes it the perfect fitness activity and hobby. Which leads to the question – why aren't more of us doing it already?

Many women report that their main objection to exercise – cycling included – is that it makes you sweat and messes up your hair.

There persists a maddening belief that sweating is somehow unfeminine. Research and surveys show time and time again that from a very young age girls begin to shy away from exercise for fear of breaking a sweat or getting a hair out of place, preferring to remain decorative onlookers. Not for nothing did the US Surgeon General issue a call in 2011 for American women to worry less about messing up their hair and more about getting active.

'Women don't sweat, they glow', the saying goes. Rubbish. Kristin Armstrong didn't get where she is today by simply 'glowing' and neither did Victoria Pendleton. Both have shed blood, sweat, tears and a lot more sweat to achieve their dreams, and I defy anybody to argue that these two women are anything but feminine.

There is no such thing as sweat-free exercise. Even walking, pilates and yoga, stereotypically very ladylike activities, will see you work up a sweat – if you don't, you're not doing it properly. Sweating means you are working your body, and it will reward you with greater fitness, clearer skin and better health. There is nothing unfeminine about it.

Below: Embrace sweating as part of a healthy lifestyle – your body will thank you for it.

Dressing for cycling

For everyday cycling you need very little in the way of proper 'kit'. As long as you're comfortable, you can cycle in pretty much anything. Wide-leg trousers and bootcut jeans may snag in your chain, so pick up a cute cycling cuff to secure your trousers to your leg. Earn extra safety points by going for a reflective or hi-vis cuff. If you can walk and bend your knees in it, you can probably cycle in it. The only items that are really off limits are extremely tight pencil-fit skirts and long dresses. You will struggle to cycle in anything too restrictive of your legs, and as an additional lack of bonus the entire street will probably be able to see your knickers/panties. Pack a pencil skirt or maxi dress into your bag if you want to wear one when you arrive and put on shorts and/or leggings for the journey.

The only other consideration with everyday clothing is the materials. As we've established, you'll probably work up a bit of a sweat while cycling and synthetic fabrics may make matters worse as they don't allow your skin to breathe. Go for natural cotton, bamboo or merino instead, (see 'base layer' opposite) or cycle in a cotton or bamboo t-shirt and get changed once you arrive. In winter, it might be tempting to throw on a thick sweater or hoodie, but if it rains or you find yourself getting overheated, these can become very heavy, soggy and take an age to dry out. Choose a lightweight fleece instead.

See Chapter Five for more ideas on cycling fashion and cycling in your everyday clothes. Once you get hooked, or start cycling more regularly and really incorporating it into your everyday life, you might want to think about investing in some basic, and not so basic, items:

Underwear

You don't need a hardcore sports bra for cycling unless you're planning on doing some serious off-roading, but you do need support and you certainly don't need underwiring digging into you while you're pedalling up a hill. Go for a medium-support sports bra or crop-top.

I have seen plenty of women cycling in thong underwear (see 'a word on leggings and tights', opposite). I personally can't think of any item of clothing I would want to wear for cycling less than a thong. Ordinary knickers/panties with a cotton gusset are absolutely fine for cycling.

Base layer

These amazing pieces of clothing, which come in long, short and sleeveless versions, keep you cool when things warm up, and warm you up when things cool down. You can buy base layers from most sports shops and from specialist cycling and sport websites.

Ideally, look for a base layer in merino. This light, soft material naturally draws sweat away from the skin and towards the outer layer of the fabric, allowing it to evaporate more easily. This process, known as 'wicking', will help keep you fresh no matter how hot and bothered you get. There are numerous brands on the market that make synthetic materials that 'wick' sweat for a similar effect, but merino is the daddy.

Base layers are functional rather than fashionable. They are designed to be worn underneath your top, sweater or jacket, so most are made in plain or neutral colours and designs. Your base layer should fit comfortably and snugly.

Leggings

These little beauties will keep your legs snug and warm against the wind and the chill, but won't weigh you down or cause you to sweat excessively. They also won't snag in your chain like ordinary trousers. You can make do with cheap fashion leggings, but proper running or cycling tights or leggings are a great investment. The materials are more suitable for sport and physical activity, with sweat-wicking and antibacterial properties. There are plenty of different finishes available too – matt, sheen or patterned – to suit fashionistas. Wear them by themselves or throw a dress, pair of shorts or a skirt on top.

Cycling-specific tights or leggings often come with padding around the seat. This is very much for comfort – and those who use them often swear by them. However, padded tights really can't double up as a fashion accessory. They are not flattering, I won't lie to you. If you fancy a bit of extra padding but don't want to look like you're wearing a giant nappy/diaper, put a pair of shorts on top.

A word on leggings and tights

Ladies, I'll be frank. The general public does not need to see your knickers/panties – unless you are blessed with the kind of endless legs and peachy bottom a supermodel would covet. Before you hop aboard your bike clad in leggings or opaque tights, do yourself a favour and take a look in the mirror in harsh lighting. VPL just isn't a good look. Fashion leggings and tights in particular often don't offer the coverage required and the usual solution to VPL, a thong, is not appropriate here unless you want to literally bare your cheeks to the world. Pop a pair of shorts or a skirt over

What I wear 'There are some specialist websites that sell clothes for women who cycle and I've bought some really practical and stylish things from them. Otherwise, I just modify my own clothes a bit. Dresses are fine – but I put a pair of shorts underneath if it's a short dress. Cycling in heels or flip-flops is OK for short journeys, but I wear trainers for longer distances.' – **Laura, 33**

the top, or team leggings with a longer-length t-shirt or vest that fully covers your rump, and your problem is solved and your dignity intact!

Waterproof trousers

Unless you are lucky enough to live in a climate where the sun always shines, waterproof trousers are a must. There is nothing pleasant about a soggy backside. Look for a style with drawstring bottoms to stop you from snagging your trouser leg in your chain. Buy a pair a size larger than you usually wear so that you can just throw them on over your outfit in the event of an unexpected shower. When not in use, roll them up and pop them in your cycling bag.

Jacket

A lightweight waterproof jacket will protect you against unexpected downpours. Choose a style cut longer at the back, to avoid soggy-bum syndrome should you happen across a few puddles. There are some fabulous cycling jackets available with clever reflective panels and trims, so you can stay safe without having to opt for hi-vis. Of course, if you want to channel your inner raver, go fluro and proud! A good cycling jacket will fold up nice and small, to stow away safely in your bag if the sun does choose to make an appearance. You can layer up underneath a waterproof jacket, so you don't need to splash out on a winter cycling jacket.

Bag

There are three main options – messenger bags, rucksacks or panniers (bags you carry on a rack fitted to the back of your bike).

Messenger bags

They are ideal if you do not have much to carry. You can easily fit your make-up, a spare top and a pair of high heels in them, then just sling them on and hop on your bike. Options range from sporty canvas bags to beautiful leather satchels.

Rucksacks

They're practical and functional, and easy to carry without weighing you down too much. Most have the capacity to carry a change of clothes, shoes and make-up, and the load is evenly distributed, avoiding any back strain. The downside of rucksacks is that a sweaty back is inevitable. Wear a base layer in a quick-drying fabric so you're not faced with soggy clothes for the return journey.

Panniers

These hook straight onto a bike rack so that you don't have to bear the additional weight on your back. You will have to buy a rack and have it fitted as most new bikes are not fitted with a rack as standard. There are many pretty designs and styles of pannier available, including double panniers for bigger loads. However, a rack and panniers will weigh the back of your bike down and may make you slower.

Small loads

For smaller loads, you can buy cute bags that attach to your handlebars or behind the saddle of your bike. If you have a shopper, you can also fit a basket to the handlebars of your bike. Just be careful about carrying anything valuable in the basket in open view, such as your handbag or purse. It's quite easy for thieving hands to dip in and snatch your belongings as you cruise past.

Gloves

Gloves help provide grip. Don't underestimate how slippery your handlebars might get in the rain or if you get a bit hot and sweaty. They also provide padding and protection for your hands, which actually work rather hard when you're cycling, especially if you're trying to work up a bit of speed. If you do take a tumble, your natural instinct is usually to put a hand out to cushion your fall, so gloves can help prevent scrapes, cuts and bruises. The elements – rain, wind, sun – are hard on your hands, which become very exposed while gripping those handlebars. Gloves protect

This page: A small handlebar bag is perfect for carrying your keys, purse and other essentials.

This page and opposite:
A hi-vis sash or vest will help motorists and other road-users spot you from a mile off.

your hands and help stop your skin drying out. A cheap pair from a local budget store just won't cut it in anything but the mildest of weather, and there is nothing more likely to make you unhappy and uncomfortable than cold, wet hands. Be kind to your hands and invest in at least one pair of functional cycling gloves.

For the colder months, layer up. Top a thinner pair with thicker fleece or waterproof gloves that you can easily slip off if things heat up.

Hi-vis

The fashion credentials of hi-vis are sketchy at best, although a fluro jacket is very nu-rave.

The safety credentials of hi-vis, however, cannot be ignored. The golden rule of safe cycling, as we have established, is that you must be seen. Hi-vis may not always make fashion sense, but it is simply common sense.

If in doubt, go out in your car (or a taxi) at dusk and look for cyclists. See the well-protected, safe cyclists in their hi-vis? Of course you do. See the 'ninjas', clad in top to toe black, gliding silently out of the gloom? Nope – not until you're practically on top of them. It's truly terrifying how invisible cyclists can be without lights and hi-vis reflective clothing.

The obvious solution is a fluorescent jacket, but if you don't want to channel your inner Bob the Builder, invest in a hi-vis sash. You can simply pop it over your outfit when you hop on your bike, and take it off once you've reached your final destination.

On your feet

You don't need special shoes for cycling. Any pair of trainers or flats will do. Trainers are more supportive and comfortable, and a pair with a textured sole can help provide grip on the pedals.

It's fine to cycle in high heels for short journeys. However, they are not terribly practical for longer stints. Carry your heels in your bag instead and pop a pair of flats on for the journey.

You can buy cycling-specific shoes for clipless pedals. Known as 'cleats', these shoes attach firmly to the pedal and help the cyclist build speed by providing greater power. As a beginner or a recreational cyclist, you absolutely do not need clipless pedals and cleats. They are an optional extra for performance and by no means essential.

What I wear 'I started off cycling in my ordinary clothes. As I got more into it I invested in a few basics – a base layer for winter, a waterproof jacket and some running tights to wear under shorts or skirts. My top buy was a pair of red and white leather fingerless cycling gloves with 'love' and 'hate' stitched across the knuckles. Very punk chic!' – **Faith, 28**

This page: Keep cool in the summer with light fabrics and bare legs.

The cycling year

The different seasons bring different pleasures and challenges when cycling. So how do you stay comfortable and confident rain or shine?

Dressing for spring

Is there a lovelier season than spring? After the long, dark, cold winter, those first few hazy days when the sun finally makes an appearance are a little slice of heaven. Spring is when the world comes alive again. Colour and light seep into our lives, and everybody feels happier and more positive with the prospect of summer just around the corner.

But springtime weather is unpredictable. Patchy sunlight and plenty of showers present challenges for the cyclist. Layering is the best approach to take as the weather gradually warms up. Start with a base layer and leggings, then you can add and remove layers as you need.

Look out for t-shirts and tops made from bamboo, a very soft fabric that has natural sweat-wicking properties and will help keep you cool, fresh and dry. A merino sweater is a good investment to keep you warm if things cool down or you need to throw on an extra layer. If you feel like really splashing out, go for a merino–cashmere mix for the ultimate in sports luxe.

Dressing for summer

It's all about keeping cool when the heat is on. In the summer, less is definitely more. Think strappy cotton vests, floaty skirts or fitted shorts, hotpants and summer dresses. It's time to show off those fantastic legs, honed from pedalling. Don't shy away from short skirts, but pop a pair of shorts on underneath to preserve your dignity. If you love a maxi, either knot the skirt above your knee to stop it trailing into your chain, or pack it in your bag to change into once you arrive.

Linen, cotton and bamboo are your friends in summer. Stay away from sweat-inducing synthetic fabrics and keep it natural.

Carry a showerproof jacket and a light merino cardigan in your cycling bag, to throw on if the temperature dips, and don't forget your sunglasses!

Dressing for autumn

Things get cooler, darker and a bit windier in autumn, but don't rule out an Indian summer either. Layering comes into its own again here. A base layer will keep you warm and dry, and you can add cotton and bamboo tops and tees.

Things can also get a bit damper in the autumn. Pack waterproof trousers in your cycling bag to protect you against the dreaded soggy bum. Keep your waterproof jacket with you at all times. You never know when you might need it. Waterproof socks can help keep your feet warm and dry. Team them with waterproof trousers on top or secure your trousers with a cycling cuff, or you might find that the rain just dribbles down your leg and collects inside the socks!

Dressing for winter

The most difficult season by far. When it's cold outside, the temptation is to wrap up very warm, but after five minutes on your bike, you're pouring sweat underneath thick, heavy clothes! What's a girl to do? Layer, layer, layer! Choose a long-sleeved base layer for winter. Layer up with long-sleeved tops, light sweaters and chunkier knits, but choose items that aren't too fiddly to remove when you are out and about. A fleece jumper is a perfect winter cycling staple. Fleece keeps you snug and warm but dries very easily if you encounter rain or work up a particularly enthusiastic sweat.

If you have enough layers on, you shouldn't need a hardcore winter jacket. Your usual waterproof will keep you dry. If you live in a climate where snow is frequent, or heavy, you might want a tougher, more durable weatherproof winter jacket. Choose something with a higher collar, to protect your neck, and a longer back.

Things get a lot darker in winter, so make sure you are covered with hi-vis and reflective strips and your bike is lit up like Times Square. When the temperature really plunges, a scarf or snood will help keep your neck and ears warm. You can also pop a thin beanie on under your cycling helmet if you're getting chilly up top. Extend the layering approach to your gloves too. You may need more than one pair, and a few lighter layers are better than thick thermal gloves, which may restrict your

Below: Don't let cold weather put you off. Wrap up warm and enjoy it!

ability to brake or use gears. Frozen face? Channel your inner bad girl and pop a balaclava on.

Eating for cycling

As we've established, cycling is fantastic exercise. If you plan on cycling regularly, you certainly don't need to worry about watching what you eat – within reason of course! In fact, cycling will burn up a lot of energy and calories. A few tweaks to your approach to eating will help you maintain your energy levels. It's better to eat foods that will keep your energy and blood sugar levels stable than to go for 'diet', low-fat, low-carb, high-sugar options, then tuck into half a chocolate cake because you're starving and need energy, now.

The basic principles of a normal, healthy, balanced approach to eating apply here. Firstly, embrace carbohydrates. They are your friends. The ongoing fad for low-carb, high-protein diets has no place here. Carbohydrates are essential for energy, to keep your blood sugar levels stable and to stop you experiencing highs and lows in blood sugar that leave you craving the empty calories found in junk food. Choose wholegrain carbohydrates wherever possible – brown rice, brown pasta and brown bread are all just as nice as white, and far better for you.

Secondly, remember protein. It's important for energy. Fish, white meat, red meat – it's all good. Red meat gets something of a bad press. While it is higher in saturated fat than fish and white meat, it's an excellent source of iron, which is vital for energy. Choose leaner cuts if you're worried about your fat intake. If you really can't get into red meat, choose chicken thighs instead of breast, as the darker meat contains more iron and zinc. If you eat a meat-free diet, good sources of protein include nuts, dairy and pulses/legumes.

Eat a rainbow of fruit and vegetables and don't forget your iron-rich leafy greens. Without enough iron you will feel lethargic and sluggish, and no amount of exercise will perk you up.

As ever, keep the fatty, sugary, starchy treats as just that – treats, not breakfast, lunch and dinner. You certainly don't need to deprive yourself unnecessarily, but if you rationalize that you 'deserve' a treat after every single cycle, you will be undoing a lot of your good work.

Carry a couple of snacks in your bag with you should you find yourself with a particularly long journey ahead and need some quick energy. Nuts, fruit, a healthy-option snack bar or some malt loaf are all ideal for an energy boost and won't fill you up and weigh you down too much. Sometimes, however, only chocolate will do!

If you only make one change to your eating habits, make it breakfast. Wholegrain toast and peanut butter, muesli, yoghurt, eggs or even just a banana are better than nothing. Many people skip breakfast because they are too busy, they are trying to lose weight or they simply do not fancy food in the morning. But having breakfast is a habit your body will thank you for. Just don't go down the sugar-loaded cereal or gigantic sugar-stuffed muffin or chocolate-chip cookie route. You will end up starving hungry at 11 am after a blood sugar crash.

Always consult your doctor before making any radical changes to your food intake, particularly if you have allergies or a condition such as diabetes that is regulated with a specific diet.

While cycling can help you manage your weight, if you have issues in that area, it is not a ticket to eating whatever you want whenever you want. No amount of exercise can counteract the harmful effects of a diet high in saturated fat, sugar and additives. If you have a difficult relationship with food, you may find embracing a healthier lifestyle easier once you have begun cycling, as it can give you the motivation to look after your body better.

Above: You don't need to make dramatic changes to your diet to keep yourself fuelled up for cycling – just keep it healthy and balanced.

But if you think changing your eating habits is impossible, don't assume you can't cycle. Consult your doctor first, but unless you have dramatic issues with food, it's usually better to cycle and eat badly than to eat badly and not exercise at all. If you cover serious mileage on your bike, expect your appetite to increase. Sticking to a healthy diet as outlined in this section will help give you the energy for cycling, but if you find yourself feeling far more tired than usual, or lacking in energy, talk to your doctor or a nutritionist for more advice on eating for cycling.

Looking after your body

Jane Wake,
leading UK fitness expert

Cycling is an excellent aerobic workout in itself. To stay in tip-top shape and cut down on the risk of exercise-induced injuries, think about your posture and incorporate some simple stretches into your routine.

Jane Wake is a leading UK fitness expert with 22 years' experience, a masters degree in sports management and a client list crammed full of celebrities, top-level athletes and blue chip companies. Here she shares her top tips, advice and exercises for cyclists, explaining how being mindful of your position and using cycling correct technique can protect you against injury and will make you faster and more efficient on your bike.

To keep your back in good cycling condition

'The best way to keep yourself injury free and cycling comfortably is to use a "neutral spine". This means holding your spine in its natural curves. Doing so places your back in its strongest position where the tension and balance of muscles is at its best. If you can then strengthen your muscles in this position, you could be comfortably touring on your bike for hours on end without any adverse effects.

'Keep moving your back as much as you can – a non-flexible back makes it harder to hold correct positions. Try yoga, Pilates and back health-focused exercise.

'To hold a neutral spine position, sit with a tall spine on your bike with your chest coming forward rather than down on the handlebars and your tailbone extended behind you. Use the top of your handlebars rather than low racing positions, keep your shoulders drawn back and down and your abdominal muscles drawn in.

'Aim for a position where you can look ahead without with your chin drawn in. Sticking your chin out to look up will shorten the back of the neck and cause tension in your upper back and shoulders.

'Use your core – drawing in through your core muscles will not only make you more stable on your bike but also save your back from strain.

Think of your core muscles not just as your abs but the inner unit of muscles that keeps your spine neutral and body in balance. Think of a drawing-up sensation from the balls of your feet, through your groin pulling up through your centre, hips gently pressed forward. Lift your entire belly up underneath your rib cage and up and out through the top of your head. At the same time, keep drawing your shoulders back and down and your chin drawn in, eyes looking straight ahead.

Cycling technique

'If you cycle in normal shoes as opposed to cleats, it's all too easy to use the push down section of a cycling motion and never the pull back. Research has shown that pro cyclists who work on the pull-back motion are not only more efficient and faster, but also less likely to have injuries. By just pushing through the balls of your feet, you are using the quadricep muscles at the front of the thigh. These are already really strong and tight, as we use them all the time in general activity. Using them without any other emphasis in cycling will make them even tighter and create bigger imbalances with other muscles, which in turn can lead to injury.

'Focus on the pull back – this is the part where your pedal hits the bottom of a cycling motion and then draws back and up. On a clock face, think of going from 4 to 12. To focus on it more, think of dragging your foot back and up, and feel your calf and hamstring muscles at the back of your leg working.'

Right: Use your core muscles to remain balanced on your bike and protect your back, and keep your shoulders back.

Stretching those cycling muscles

It's important to stretch regularly to stop your muscles becoming tight and uncomfortable. Pilates or yoga are great additions to your exercise routine and will help keep your muscles strong. Alternatively, try the stretches and exercises Jane has suggested, right, to look after your body when you're not in the saddle.

Aim to stretch out most days – in the evening after a hot bath and in front of the TV is ideal. Stretch the leg muscles, particularly the front thigh but also the hamstrings, calves and gluteal muscles in the bum and hip. Your back and shoulders also need a good stretch. Hold each stretch for at least a minute, relax and breathe out as you stretch.

1 Strengthening your core muscles
Resting on your hands and knees, adopt a neutral spine – hands in line with shoulders, knees in line with hips, small curve in your lower back. Bend your elbows slightly and tuck them in – imagine you are holding a pencil underneath each armpit. Keep looking down at the floor, just above your fingertips – your upper body should already feel as though it is working. Next, curl your toes under so that you can rest on the balls of your feet and carefully lift your knees off the floor. Focus on keeping your core muscles drawn in and maintain your neutral spine position.

2 Lying hamstring and calf stretch
Lie on your back on the floor and place a towel or band underneath your right foot, then slowly extend your leg up to the ceiling. Hold for 3–6

slow breaths. Focus on pressing your heel to the ceiling and your tailbone to the floor and feel the stretch in your calf. Repeat with the other leg.

can't reach, use your band or towel. Keeping your hips pressed into the floor, gently bring your heel up towards your bottom. Hold for 3–6 slow breaths, then repeat with the other leg.

3 Lying hip and bum stretch

Place your band or towel around your left thigh and cross your right lower leg over your left thigh. Holding onto the band with your left hand, slowly lift the left foot off the floor as you gently press your right knee out with your right hand. Keep your bottom on the floor and your tummy in. You should feel a stretch in your right buttock. Hold for 3–6 slow breaths, then change sides.

5 Knealing chest, neck and back stretch

From a kneeling position, place your left hand and forearm onto a low stool or chair. With your elbow at right angles, gently press your body down and away from your left side, looking towards the right until you feel a gentle stretch in your chest and neck. Hold for 3–6 slow breaths and change sides. Draw your shoulder blade down as you slowly turn away from your arm.

4 Lying front thigh and hip stretch

Lie onto your front, resting your head into your left hand. Take a hold of your right foot – if you

looking ⁵
good
while
cycling

Thanks to the revolution in women's cycling, it's almost impossible not to look great on two wheels.

Bikes customized by the likes of Diane von Furstenberg, Betsey Johnson and Isaac Mizrahi available for hire at New York Fashion Week. Cycling accessories designed by Henry Holland and Giles Deacon at London Fashion Week. Gucci and Chanel designing their own bikes – the latter complete with a trademark quilted saddle. Pashley Poppy bicycles popping up in high-fashion glossy magazine shoots. Fixed-wheel bicycles replacing skinny lattes and glasses without lenses as the accessory of choice for the discerning hipster. Cycling has never been hotter property, more stylish or more fashionable.

And it has also become the preserve of the stylish, with many leading fashionistas only too happy to sing cycling's praises. TV presenter Dawn Porter is a super-keen cyclist, telling the London Cycle Chic blog: 'I am addicted to my bike! I would never be able to fit so much into the day with such little stress without it.' She advises fashion-conscious cyclistas to: 'Pick a colour and go with it – for me, it's all about pink!' Supermodel Elle 'The Body' MacPherson is another cyclist with serious fashion credentials. She told media gathered at a Skyride launch: 'I cycle as much as I can, whether I'm in the centre of London or getting away from the city.' She added: 'You don't have to be an Olympic champion to cycle. Get out there and enjoy the environment!'

Cycling has been embraced by just about everybody who is anybody. Vanessa Hudgens, the epitome of Young Hollywood, is often spotted on her bicycle, as is global superstar Katy Perry. Even the Material Girl herself, Madonna, has been photographed on a sleek silver mountain bike cruising around London and heading to Abbey Road studios to record.

How did we come to this happy state of affairs? How has cycling shot from geek to chic?

For many years, sports and cycling shops stocked a small range of functional, fairly unlovable bikes, accessories and clothes for women, in amongst reams and reams of bikes, accessories and clothes for men. Women who wanted to cycle didn't have a great deal of choice available to them. They could don the

Above and below: From sporty chic to catwalk, cycling is as versatile as it is accessible.

Opposite page: High fashion on two wheels – cycling at its stylish best.

dreary and unflattering Lycra garments designed for men. Or they could make do with their own clothes, without the technical fabrics and nifty innovations we discussed in the last chapter.

Fortunately, some early pioneers of what has come to be known as the 'cycle chic' movement were not too happy with this state of affairs. One such pioneer is Amy Fleuriot, fashion designer and founder of British label Cyclodelic. Like many of us, Amy cycled a lot in her active youth. When she began studying accessories at the London College of Fashion, she borrowed her mum's old bike to get to work. Soon her eye was caught by the small but growing fixed-wheel movement in London and cycling became a lifestyle choice rather than a simple method of transport.

Combining her passion for cycling with her passion for fashion, Amy launched Cyclodelic in 2006 as an events brand. Products including beautiful cycling bags, capes and tunics followed in 2009 and then came a concession at fashion mecca Topshop in London's Oxford Circus – a defining moment for the cycling chic movement. This marked the first occasion that stylish women's cycling had crossed over into the mainstream.

'There were hardly any women cycling when I started – and if there were, they were head to toe in Lycra. I didn't have any role models or anybody I could ride with and ask for advice. I still remember the first time I headed out in the evening on my bike, on my way home from university. My classmates were horrified! They all said: "You can't cycle at night!" I felt so brave, dressed head to toe in fluro, it was like I was putting on the uniform of a warrior.'
– Amy Fleuriot, fashion designer and founder of Cyclodelic

Meanwhile, websites sourcing and selling beautiful cycling clothes and accessories were beginning to spring up. Some were accompanied by blogs offering tips and advice on looking good on two wheels. Fashion and lifestyle magazines began to sit up and take notice, as did newspapers, and soon products from Cyclodelic and websites like Cyclechic were appearing in glossy shoots and spreads labelled as 'lust-haves'.

The most successful websites and brands stock products that are a crossover between functional and performance-orientated cycling gear and fashion accessories. Bags are designed to be fitted to the handlebars or saddle of your bike – and look great while they are on there. Tunics, t-shirts and bespoke cycling dresses are made from bamboo, merino and cotton combined with performance fabrics like Lycra, offering the wearer the best of technical fabrics with a high-fashion twist. Jackets feature reflective piping and panels to aid visibility without going down the high-vis road. A great deal of cycling fashion has a slightly vintage aesthetic – tweed or rain capes, herringbone or faux fur helmet covers, ditsy 50s-style floral printed panniers. For those who are not fans of the super-pretty look, bold colours, simple clean lines and brilliant functionality feature heavily on many cycling-specific products. Whatever your style, you can also find plenty to suit you. Here are some of the best brands to look out for. You will find a directory of sites at the back of the book.

Basil

This great brand from the spiritual home of cycling, the Netherlands, is best known for its range of beautiful cycling bags and panniers. The products have a vintage, retro feel. Think cute baskets for your handlebars and ditsy floral-print panniers. Basil also makes a great range of pet baskets for bikes – the only thing that could possibly make a vintage shopper more desirable is a puppy in the basket!

Bobbin

Initially a manufacturer of beautiful vintage upright bicycles with a practical modern twist, Bobbin has now branched out into accessories. With stylish leather panniers with a bit of a Sherlock Holmes vibe, cycling capes and brilliant helmets in precious metal tones, the look is sophisticated, retro and endlessly British.

Cyclodelic

London label Cyclodelic is famed for its stunning range of cycling bags and accessories. Handlebar or saddle bags come in hot pink, zebra print and lipstick red to name but a few, making them the ultimate in tough yet feminine chic. Founder Amy Fleuriot is a renowned designer with an infectious passion for cycling. She has even customized fixed-wheel bikes, turning basic machines into super-covetable works of art. Her collection also includes clothing and cycling accessories that combine fashion with performance.

Sawako Furuno

Tokyo-born, London-based Sawako Furuno, a trained architect, has achieved the seemingly impossible – a range of helmets so beautiful they make staying safe positively stylish. The fash pack raves about her amazing designs. A range of products such as jackets are in the pipeline too, which, if they are anything like the helmets, will be an instant cult hit.

Terry

Founded by Georgena Terry in 1985, this US women's cycling brand sells clothes, bikes and accessories that combine style with performance. The site also sources the best of cycling fashion from other labels, ranging from high-end outdoor wear brand North Face to hip shoe designers Fly London. Not just about the products themselves, the brand also supports cycling and charity events to get more women on their bikes.

YMX

US sportswear brand YMX makes a range of traditional cycling jerseys in very untraditional prints and patterns. The range is colourful and eye-catching, with solid performance credentials. Its imagery is inspired by artistic cultures from around the world, including Chinese and Celtic tattoo styles, and is designed to flatter the female form to the maximum.

Above, top and bottom:
Beautiful cycling accessories combine style with substance and practicality.

Sombrio

This Canadian brand sums up the ethos and style of mountain biking. Tough yet chic hoodies, tank tops and shorts suit sporty cyclistas who, as the brand itself says 'may have pink nails, but there is often dirt under them'.

Rapha

British road cycling brand Rapha is beloved by elite cyclists for its technical fabrics and high-performance products. In fact, the world's highest ranked cycling team, Team Sky, has chosen Rapha to be its official clothing provider. Its women's range has its roots in performance and is designed to make the most of the female form.

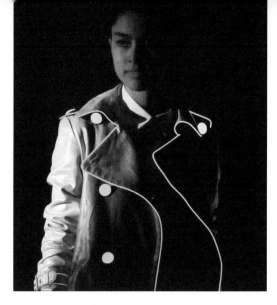

Above: Clever reflective trim means you don't have to go hi-vis to be seen.

Knog

Best known for making cute and cool lights that are just as easy to attach to helmets, bags and clothes as they are bikes, Aussie brand Knog also makes stylish messenger bags and must-have cycling gloves. Even its range of bike locks is bright, bold and covetable.

Vespertine

Reflectives that double up as couture are the USP of this incredible New York brand. The range includes belts, jackets, scarves, pins and the trademark Vesperts, some of which even come with sequins. Being seen and being safe has never been so stylish.

Cyclechic

This great website, which began life as the London Cycle Chic blog, brings together the best and most beautiful products from cycling

Left: Check out Aussie manufacturer Knog for cute and functional bike lights.

brands around the world. It is particularly good for finding stylish helmets and gorgeous bags and panniers.

Minx

Another website bringing together the best from cycling fashion and performance brands around the world, including maternity cycling wear for pregnant cyclistas. Minx also encourages questions from her dedicated following and is happy to share her expert knowledge of the products.

Sweaty Betty

Many of the gorgeous workout clothes outside of the cycling range made by this British brand are perfect for life on two wheels. Check out the shrugs for keeping arms warm without overheating the rest of your body.

Velorution

A great little one-stop shop with everything you need for stylish cycling, from a bike suitable for urban commuting to bags, helmets and clothes. The brand is very London focused but has an excellent website for online shopping.

The ultimate cycling beauty regime

With a few tweaks, your daily beauty routine can easily be adapted to incorporate cycling.

Helmets and hair

If I'm honest I've never had helmet hair. I actually don't know many female cyclists who have. Neither, for that matter, does Cyclodelic's Amy Fleuriot. As the doyenne of cycling fashion, I was keen to hear her views on helmet hair and heartened to learn she also had never found it an issue. You will read plenty about helmet hair in magazine and newspaper articles and you will probably hear about it from non-cyclists. As in: 'I'd love to cycle – but I really don't want to get helmet hair.' But in my experience you won't hear many actual cyclists talking about it. In fact, helmet hair may well be one of those urban myths that all of us have heard of but none of us have actually experienced. With that caveat, if you have thin hair or a shorter style that takes a lot of upkeep and maintenance, then you might be worried about the effect of a helmet on your hair.

There are two main issues here. Firstly, helmets can get quite warm, so if you are cycling for any length of time or in nice weather, sweating can have an impact on your hair. Secondly, if you have an excessively styled barnet, a helmet might squash or flatten down the root lift you've spent all morning backcombing to achieve.

Take dry shampoo, a travel brush and your usual styling products with you if you are concerned about your hair. A quick spritz of dry shampoo should clear up any sweat issues, and you can then style your crowning glory as usual once you have arrived at your destination. If your hair is longer but prone to oiliness, beauty experts sometimes suggest working a small amount of powder into the roots to absorb any excess oil and add volume. Tie longer locks back in a ponytail or plait/braid and pop your helmet on top. These low-maintenance styles are perfectly compatible with a cycling helmet. A quick brush through when you arrive should be all you need.

Cycling and skincare

Many people notice an improvement in their skin once they begin exercising regularly. The boost in circulation helps promote a smooth, glowing complexion. A good sweat can also help to clear out pores, leaving your skin clearer.

It's important to look after your skin as cycling is an outdoor exercise and can be hard on the skin. As you will inevitably sweat more when you are cycling regularly, make sure you drink plenty of water. We are all instructed that we should aim for eight glasses a day, more if you are exercising. If this seems a bit of a regimental approach, just keep a bottle or glass of water next to you throughout the day, and you will easily get into the habit of drinking plenty. Try and drink a big glass of water as soon as you wake up, to freshen you up and get you ready for the day.

Face
Use a moisturizer with at least SPF15, and go higher if you have very fair skin or live in a very hot climate. Use it year round, not just in summer. Even when it's cold out, your face is still exposed to the elements. Outdoor exercise can be drying, so if you find your skin starting to feel tight and uncomfortable, choose a richer moisturizer for the days when you know you are going to be on your bike. You can always wash your face and re-apply your normal moisturizer once you arrive.

Some people, especially those with dry skin, find regular outdoor exercise can leave them with rosy cheeks. Choose an anti-redness moisturizer to help neutralize your skin tone. Or simply go easy on the blusher! If your skin is on the oily side, don't neglect the moisturizer. Choose an oil-free or mattifying complex instead.

Arms, legs and shoulders

Slather on at least SPF15 before you head out on your bike with your limbs or shoulders exposed. You might not feel the heat of the sun as you will generate a cool breeze while cycling, but many a cyclist has been caught out with painfully burned shoulders after a long pleasant ride in the summer sunshine. Moisturize your skin with body or skin lotion following your post-ride shower. The fresh air can be very drying.

Hands

Even if you wear gloves, your hands still need a bit of looking after. They may become very dry, particularly around the knuckles, so moisturize regularly with a good hand cream. If you are not wearing gloves, use a barrier cream on your hands before you cycle.

Make-up

If you can bear it, it's better to cycle bare faced. Give your skin the chance to breathe and it will thank you for it. Embrace the liberation and enjoy the freedom of not worrying about your mascara smudging or your lipstick needing re-applying. Once you arrive, you can simply freshen up with facial wipes and a light moisturizer before applying your make-up as normal. Make the most of your natural glow and go easy on the blusher.

Going bare faced isn't for everybody, however. And if you are cycling to a social engagement, rather than to work, you might not want to take your make-up bag with you. Swap your usual base for a lighter tinted moisturizer. A heavier foundation or powder will block your pores, and if you sweat, you might find your entire face running off! A lighter option will give you coverage without the risk of arriving with your top covered in fawn streaks.

Choose waterproof mascara for the same reason. Go for a lighter eye rather than a dramatic smoky khol-rimmed look. Excessive amounts of make-up running into your eyes is never a good look.

Cycling and me

'Cycling has its own culture, and if you're wearing something that's functional and in a great colour or has a different cut to it, you look fashionable. In sport, the only time you look silly is when you're trying too hard to look normal. Be comfortable and wear the appropriate kit, but wear colours that are you. I wear my red lipstick when I ride sometimes, not because I'm afraid of people on the road seeing me without make-up, but because my red lipstick is part of me and my style, and as it doesn't affect how I ride my bike – why the hell not? Other days I ride without any make-up; it just depends on how I feel.' – Cate, 27

And if you really, really can't bear to be seen with a hair out of place...

At the end of the day, cycling has to fit in around you, not the other way around. Having read this far and taken in all the motivational pep talks about sweat being a good thing, you may still feel that you don't want to compromise on looking your best at all times. That's your prerogative and the good news is that you can still cycle and look perfect at all times. Here's how:

Take it easy
You won't get the same health and fitness benefits from a gentle pedal as you will from going all-out with gusto. But you will still get health and fitness benefits from a lower-key cycle, just as you can still get health and fitness benefits from a sedate walk. Take your time and don't push yourself too hard and the risk of sweating should be kept to an absolute minimum as a result.

Slow down for the last mile or so
Even if you're cycling very sedately, slowing to a cruise for the last mile or so of your journey should see you arrive looking and feeling as cool as a cucumber. Enjoy the gentle breeze and freewheel as much as possible.

Travel light
Take as little as possible with you, to avoid weighing down your bike and making you work harder. Choose a bag that fits onto your bike, such as a pannier, basket or handlebar bag. Avoiding rucksacks, which can make your back very hot, will help to keep you cool and calm.

Left: A shopper is the perfect bike for fashionistas. Accessorise with gorgeous panniers and a basket on the front. Take things steady if you don't want to work up too much of a sweat.

Be prepared to freshen up
Pack a small hairbrush and travel-sized deodorant, wipes, a light moisturizer, lipstick, powder and eyeshadow. That way you are always prepared should you have to touch up your look after the journey. Plan to get to your destination 10 minutes early so that you have time to freshen up.

Choose your bike accordingly
Your best option is a classic shopper: they are easy and comfortable to ride and built for style over performance. Accessorize with a basket on the handlebars, a gorgeous saddlebag or a rack and ditsy panniers, and your bike will become as much a part of your look as your bag, shoes or jewellery.

Layer it up
Keep cool in light layers. Team a pretty printed dress with a light merino cardigan for natural sweat-wicking and antibacterial (read no smell) properties. Go for a hooded waterproof that folds up nice and small to throw on in case of an unexpected shower. Alternatively, look for a waterproof cape, and rock out a vintage look.

Strap in
If you want to cycle in heels, go ahead! Just choose a pair with a strap to stop your feet sliding out. Chunkier heels are easier to cycle in than stilettoes, but as long as you're not hoping to work up any kind of speed, you really can cycle in pretty much any footwear. For longer journeys, pop on a pair of pretty ballet pumps and carry your heels in the basket to change into later.

Buy the prettiest helmet you can find
Why stop at one? When there's a choice of brands and designs ranging from Liberty-style floral prints, traditional tweeds and nu-rave hot pinks, you can have a helmet to match every outfit. Renowned New York-based fashion editor and blogger Liberty London Girl is a huge fan of helmet designer du jour Sawako Furuno. Also check out Bern, Yakkay and Bobbin for a variety of amazing styles.

Cycle-spiration

Searching for inspiration for your cycling style? Look no further than the brilliant and talented women who have made a full-time, hugely successful career out of their love of two wheels.

Victoria Pendleton

The queen of track cycling, 'VP' retired after London 2012 with fistfuls of Olympic medals and World Championships to her name. Glamorous, brilliant and touchingly vulnerable, she has achieved iconic status well outside the world of professional cycling. Her undeniable star quality makes her a once-in-a-generation athlete, and her off-track style is the definition of cycling chic. VP looks as stunning crouched over her bike in her Team GB kit in the velodrome as she does glammed up for a gorgeous photoshoot.

Get her look
On the track VP is all business. She embraces Lycra and has the incredible, gym-honed figure to pull it off to perfection. Her training kit is simple and clean. Think white tank-tops and racer-backs, laid-back hoodies and black sweatpants or cycling tights. No worries about helmet hair for Victoria; she ties her long locks back underneath her futuristic helmet.

Away from the velodrome, VP rocks vintage glamour with a twist. Steal her style with elegant full-skirted dresses nipped in at the waist, a powder-blue shopper from her own bike range and supersized sunglasses. Accessorize with big hair and a megawatt smile.

Kristin Armstrong

The First Lady of cycling has combined motherhood with a glittering road-racing career. When she's not taking the world on in her full cycling gear, Kristin is the ultimate yummy mummy. Think simple separates, a golden glow and honey-blond locks.

Get her look
Train like Kristin in patriotic tanks, racer-backs and tees. Show off tanned, toned legs in the shortest of shorts and keep the look fresh, simple and natural.

Channel her off-duty look with pastel v-necks and skinny jeans or slim-fit trousers in neutral shades. Embrace the all-American, soccer mom vibe with shiny, bouncy hair and barely-there make-up.

Laura Trott

If Victoria Pendleton is the queen of the velodrome, Laura Trott is the princess. This brilliant, up-and-coming young cyclist was part of the gold medal-winning British pursuit team at London 2012, and also went on to scoop individual gold in the omnium. And all at the tender age of 20!

Laura started the trend for patriotic nail art at the 2012 Olympics, and her trademark blonde plaits/ braids are already threatening to become iconic.

There is a great deal of expectation already riding upon her shoulders, with her potential much assessed and discussed. Expect to see a lot more of this pint-sized superstar. Laura is tough and fragile in equal measure – her health battles are well documented and she is living proof that physical adversity (she was born with a collapsed lung) is not necessarily a barrier to success.

Get her look
Laura's wholesome on-track style is given its own twist with her fondness for plaits, which double up as a functional way to keep hair in check while cycling. Outside the velodrome she

Left and below: Kristin Armstrong, left, and the gorgeous women of Team GB, below, provide the ultimate in cycling inspiration.

Above: Part of the gold-medal winning women's team pursuit team, Great Britain's Joanna Rowsell is a poster-girl for positive self image.

goes for skinny jeans or cropped trousers, simple vests and tees and well-cut blazers for a preppy, clean-cut look. She can also rock a LBD with the best of them and likes to have fun with fashion. After the Olympic Games, she and fellow Team

GB athletes dressed up as British girlband the Spice Girls for a magazine shoot, with Laura choosing to copy the bubblegum style of Emma Bunton, aka 'Baby Spice'.

Dani King

Another brilliant young British cyclist, Dani King was part of the gold-medal winning, world-record beating Team GB pursuit team at London 2012. A virtual unknown before the Olympics, Dani had overcome a bout of glandular fever that at one point looked in danger of ending her career, and is now firmly on the radar of everybody with an interest in cycling. At just 21, her future looks very bright. Dani is a naturally gifted athlete – she ran and swam at county level before switching to cycling aged 15. The rest is now history!

Super-glamorous Dani has been photographed out on the town in short shift dresses and her beautiful athletic frame, long shiny dark hair and winning smile suit simple classics. However, the ultimate cycle-spiration comes from pictures of Dani out partying in her Team GB kit, showing that it's possible to rock out in full-on Lycra and still look utterly sensational.

Get her look
Simple, clean lines look best on an athletic figure like Dani's. Show off killer legs in short skirts, but keep necklines high and demure to stay classy. Or, head out straight from cycling and party in your training kit!

Joanna Rowsell

The third member – and the heartbeat – of the gold-medal winning pursuit team, Joanna is also the most noticeable when the helmets are removed. She has alopecia and her long auburn hair fell out when she was very young. She has found confidence through her incredible cycling ability and created one of the iconic images of London 2012 when she chose to step onto the podium without a helmet or wig hiding her almost bald scalp. She credits her alopecia with giving her the drive and determination to succeed. Although she chooses to cycle au naturel underneath her helmet, she owns a selection of wigs that she mixes and matches to suit her mood and her overall look when off the track.

Get her look

Sporty Jo is most often found in training gear and tracksuits. When not on duty she favours fun, flirty, girly dresses in bright bold colours and a series of wigs for a knockout look. A genuine poster girl for self-image, Jo has said she hopes to inspire other girls with alopecia to accept themselves and be comfortable with who they are.

Sarah Storey

Great Britain's most decorated Paralympian, the legend that is Sarah Storey, is a relentless, medal-winning machine. She has beaten the best in both swimming and cycling, and narrowly missed out on selection for the London 2012 Olympic team. Although she was born without a functioning left hand, Sarah has excelled against able-bodied athletes and was the first disabled cyclist to compete for England at the Commonwealth Games. Off the track, Sarah loves classic, elegant fashion and names Karen Millen as her favourite label.

Get her look

Classic elegance never goes out of style. At 34, Sarah personifies grown-up glamour and has a weakness for beautiful accessories, shoes and bags. Team with immaculate make-up and glossy, Hollywood waves for Sarah's red-carpet bombshell style.

What all these women prove is that cycling style is about more than what you wear and how you style your hair. Cycling has given all of these women the confidence to overcome personal battles and adversity. It has empowered them to want to be the best they can possibly be, without compromising their femininity. Cycling has allowed them to succeed while remaining true to themselves.

The highly emotional Victoria Pendleton is famed for her tears after a race – tears of happiness if she wins, tears of sadness if she does not. She has proved that even those with extreme mental toughness can embrace their softer, more emotional sides and remain world-beaters. Sarah Storey has proved that physical disability can be overcome, and that talent does not discriminate. Jo Rowsell has proved that beauty can be found in many forms, and her strength and unquestionable beauty remind us that often the greatest barrier we face is the way we feel about ourselves.

Cycling and me 'The Olympics changed so much for me – watching Lizzie Armitstead and Emma Pooley on the road, and Victoria Pendleton and Laura Trott in the velodrome just did something to the way I thought about cycling, and female athletes. Having women in fitness and sport to look up to is really refreshing, and even as a 27-year-old, I still need a role model. Personally, I'd rather be looking up to a world and Olympic champion like 32-year-old Pendleton than a 20-year-old pop star. I just hope that more female athletes get the exposure they need to help inspire more young girls to consider cycling and sports as their hobby. Fitness is so important, and having young girls get to know their bodies from a sports and fitness perspective, rather than just a dieting and beauty standpoint, would help change society as we know it.' - Cate, 27

Cycling and pregnancy

Not strictly a fashion concern, but a very female one nonetheless. Should you find yourself expecting the patter of tiny feet, is it safe to carry on with your two-wheeled lifestyle?

There is no short or simple answer to this, as it very much depends upon what you personally consider acceptable when it comes to risk. Physically, as long as you are not suffering from any debilitating condition, exercise during pregnancy is actively encouraged. Always check with your doctor first. However, as long as you are fit and healthy and have no underlying conditions, your doctor should be happy for you to continue cycling.

In fact, exercise such as cycling can be hugely beneficial during pregnancy, helping your body prepare for the physical demands of childbirth. It can also help with some of the more glamorous side effects of pregnancy including constipation, varicose veins and circulation problems as well as backache. The main issue with cycling while pregnant is the risk of having an accident.

It is entirely a personal decision as to whether you continue cycling or not, and to what extent. You may want to continue as normal, you may prefer to restrict your cycling to quiet roads or off-road paths and routes only or you may want to give it a miss altogether.

If you do decide to continue cycling throughout pregnancy, be aware that once you start to develop a bump, your balance may be affected. Your body is not used to carrying so much weight in one place. You may find you have to adjust your saddle and handlebars a little as you grow. In late pregnancy you may be quite happy to cycle, or you may find your balance is too off for comfort. Again, it's personal choice, so do what feels right for you.

You may find you tire more easily when pregnant, so allow yourself extra time for your journeys and don't push yourself to the limit. Always keep a snack and a drink in your bag so that you can stop and fuel up, should you need to. However passionately you feel about cycling during your pregnancy, if your body starts telling you to slow down or stop, listen to it.

Cycling after you've had your baby is a great way to get your body back and regain some of your much-missed independence. However, don't hop back in the saddle until you're fully healed. Childbirth is a huge experience for your body to go through, so even if you're feeling fantastic after just a few days, wait until you've been given the all clear from your doctor to start cycling again. This will usually happen at your six-week post-partum checkup when, all being well, your doctor should be able to give you the go-ahead to start exercising again. Make sure you specifically ask your doctor if it's OK for you to cycle, as other forms of exercise such as walking, swimming and yoga are much lower impact. If you've had stitches or a C-section, you may have to wait a little longer. Be patient. Chances are if you have had to have surgery or stitches you'll be too sore to think about cycling for a good few months anyway!

Take it slowly when you first get back in the saddle and don't push yourself too hard. There's plenty of time to lose that baby weight.

If you want to cycle with your baby, you can buy specially designed seats to fit on your bicycle. Take note of age guidelines and discuss it with your doctor or health visitor. Newborn babies are very fragile and you won't want to be bumping your precious cargo about until he or she is strong enough physically to withstand it.

Right: Cycling can be a great way to keep active during your pregnancy, but always check with your doctor first.

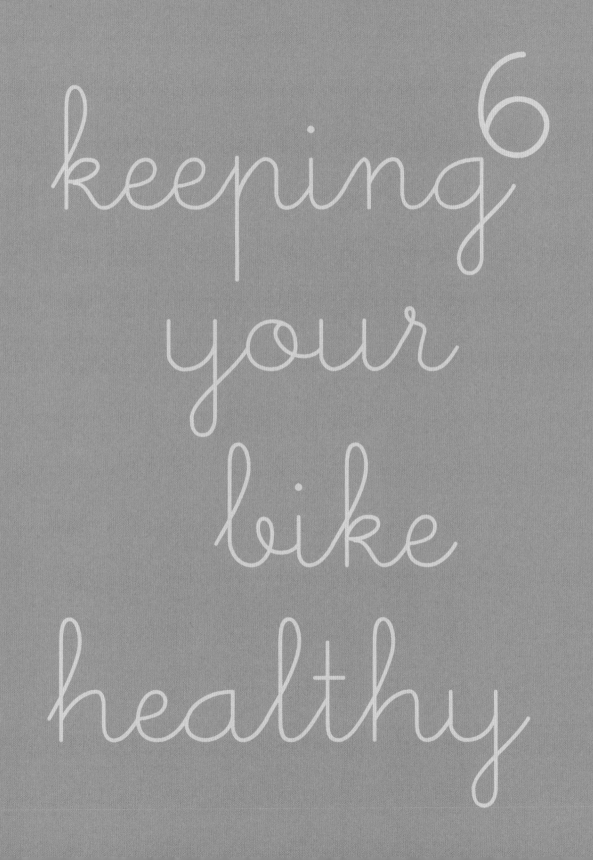

6

keeping your bike healthy

Love your bike. It's a low-maintenance piece of machinery but if you treat it kindly, it will reward you with hours of happy, easy, trouble-free cycling.

The bargainista credentials of cycling come into their own when considering maintenance. Unless you are very unlucky, the odd spare part and service at a bike shop should be all you need to shell out on.

This chapter will look at the basic maintenance you can do yourself, including checking your bike, cleaning and fixing punctures. Should you enjoy embracing your inner mechanic, there are some brilliant books, videos and resources out there that will help you learn more about bike maintenance. The directory at the back of the book will point you in the right direction.

All the advice and tips in this chapter apply to recreational cyclists using everyday bikes. Super-pricey, specialist bikes need more dedicated professional upkeep. I would recommend taking a course in bike maintenance to learn how to get the best out of your dream machine.

Essential tools of the trade

To look after your bike properly, you will need a few bits and bobs. All of the below can be bought very cheaply from a good bike shop.

Bike spanner

If your bike doesn't have quick-release wheels and saddle, you will need a spanner that fits the nuts holding your wheels and saddle in place. Choose a specialist bike spanner, which comes with several different-sized holes that should fit all the nuts and bolts on your bike.

Allen key

This L-shaped piece of metal is cut to the hexagonal shape of the screws on your bike. You will be able to buy an allen key that fits your bike at a good bike shop.

Tyre levers

Use proper tyre levers to remove tyres when changing inner tubes. You can buy plastic, nylon or metal levers, and some puncture repair kits come with them included. For recreational cycling, plastic should be fine. If you find that you consistently break the levers craning your tyre off (see pages 108–109), go for metal instead but be very careful not to damage the wheel rim or the inner tube.

Pump

You can never have too many pumps, so buy at least two – one to keep at home and one to keep in your cycling bag. There are all kinds available, from basic hand pumps to sophisticated models, all the way through to professional foot-operated pumps. As long as it blows air into your tyres, it will suffice. You can also buy canisters of compressed air to re-inflate tyres, but these are not essential. A pump will do the job fine.

Spare inner tubes

Buy two spares and keep one at home and one in your bag. As soon as you use one up, replace it immediately. That way you will never be caught short.

Puncture repair kit

These nifty little kits contain everything you need to fix a puncture, including patches, adhesive and chalk. They are very cheap and super small so it's easy to carry one around with you.

Chain lubricant

Your bike chain needs to be kept clean and well lubricated so that it can continue to function properly. You can buy specialist chain lubricants, which tend to be more expensive than your bog-standard oil. These technical mixtures help keep the chain clean and in tip-top condition. For recreational cycling, basic bike oil is fine.

Cleaning equipment

There are all sorts of fancy bike cleaning products, degreasers and cleaning accessories on the market. As a recreational cyclist, you don't need to splash out unless you really want to. You can make do with a sponge and some basic bike wash. To clean your chain thoroughly you will need a small brush. You can either buy one or use an old toothbrush.

Your bike maintenance calendar

As a general rule, the more you use your bike the more you will need to look after it. Taking a few minutes to check your bike on a regular basis, and giving it a good clean when it's starting to look a bit grubby, will keep your bike in good working order and help you spot any issues or problems before they become serious.

Checking your bike

Check your bike thoroughly at least once a month, more if you cycle regularly or cover serious distances. Start at the front of your bike and work backwards.

Front wheel and brake

Begin with the front wheel. Ensure the tyre is hard and fully inflated. Soft, deflated tyres make cycling more difficult and arduous, and increase the risk of punctures and damage to the wheels. Press the tyre firmly with your thumbs. You should not be able to depress the tyre at all and it should feel rock hard, not spongy or giving. If you feel any give in the tyre at all, pump it up.

Next, lift the front of the bike off the ground and spin the front wheel. Check that it is running easily and not catching against either brake pad. Look for any damage to the rims or wear to the tyres. If you can see the threads of the tyres, it's time to replace them.

Give the wheel a gentle shake, to check that it is firmly held in position. Tighten up the fastenings if necessary. Spin the wheel and apply the front brake. The brake should stop the wheel rotating immediately with light to medium pressure. A certain amount of wear on the brakes is inevitable, but if you have to fully apply the brake to stop the wheel, then it is too loose and you will need to tighten it or replace the brake pads.

Check the front brake pads are even and not too worn down. A certain amount of wear is acceptable, but they should not be worn down to the point that they do not make full contact with the wheel rim. The front brake cable should show no signs of fraying.

Handlebars

Standing in front of your bike and facing it, grip the front wheel firmly between your legs. Give the handlebars a gentle rock. They should be secure and not twist or rotate. If the handlebars are loose, it can affect your steering. (See page 111 for guidance on tightening your handlebars.)

Frame

Run an eye over the bike frame. Look out for cracks and rust. Cracks in the frame or heavy rusting could be a sign of serious damage and should be seen to immediately. It helps if your bike is clean when you check the frame.

Pedals

The pedals should rotate freely and be securely fixed. Lift the rear of the bike and turn the pedals to check they are running smoothly. Give them a gentle rock to ensure they are not loose. Bent or damaged pedals should be repaired or replaced by a bike mechanic or at your local bike shop.

Chain

Rotate the pedals and watch the chain moving along the hubs. It should move freely and quietly. Clicking, slipping and squeaking can indicate a problem and a trip to the bike shop is in order. See pages 104–105 for advice on chain maintenance.

Gears

Look for any rust or damage to the gear hubs and derailleur, if your bike has one. Check everything is clean and running smoothly and there are no ominous clicks or creaks. Slipping gears need professional attention immediately.

Saddle

Give the saddle a good twist. It should remain secure and not budge. If it twists to the left or the right, you need to tighten up the fastening holding the saddle in place (see page 111).

Rear wheel and brake

Check the rear tyre, wheel, brake and brake cable in exactly the same way as you checked the front.

Lights

Check your lights are working fully on all settings. Change the batteries as soon as they begin to dim or the flashing patterns become erratic.

Cleaning your bike

Give your bike a thorough clean at least once a month. Coincide it with carrying out the checks above and you can have all your bike maintenance done and dusted in one go. It's important to keep your bike clean for several reasons. Firstly, it will keep it looking gorgeous, which is actually not

just a superficial concern. If your bike looks great and makes you happy, you will be more likely to use it more often, and take better care of and greater pride in it.

Secondly, keeping your bike clean will help keep it running smoothly and extend its shelf life. Dirty bikes that are frequently left damp and covered in filth rust quickly, and once rust has set in its bye bye bike. Dirty chains in particular are prone to rusting, clicking, cracking, breaking and generally causing no end of problems. Grubby reflectors and lights don't do their job properly, potentially putting you in danger.

No excuses here! If you don't have access to a garden and/or a hose pipe, take your bike out onto the pavement/sidewalk or into a local park and clean it there with a sponge and bucket. Even taking it to a garage to give it a quick spray with the jet wash is better than nothing.

It's best to use proper bike wash or bike cleaner, or even car shampoo, but if you are watching the pennies, you can make do with ordinary washing-up liquid. This isn't ideal as it doesn't protect the frame, as some of the more advanced bike cleaners do, and can be harsh and abrasive. Washing-up liquids and general detergents also contain a lot of salt, which can lead to rust if you don't rinse properly. Bike purists would be horrified to hear me advocating washing-up liquid but it's still better than a grubby bike.

Cleaning your bike the professional way

Firstly, spray your bike with degreaser and leave for 30 seconds, or according to the instructions on the product. Use a soft brush to scrub at any particularly stubborn patches of filth. Then rinse your bike thoroughly.

Next, wash the entire bike with bike or car shampoo diluted in warm water. Use a soft cloth or a specialist bike brush to scrub off any dirt that remains. Rinse your bike thoroughly, ideally with warm water. Polish with a chamois leather or a soft dry cloth.

Finally, clean the chain. Remove the entire chain and soak it in white spirit or a professional chain cleaner. Clean the gear hubs and derailleur with degreaser, using a specialist brush or toothbrush to get into every single cog. Once the chain has soaked, rinse it thoroughly and hang it up to dry. Ensure it is completely dry before lubricating and replacing.

Cleaning your bike the Girl's Guide way

Read that thinking 'Whew, that sounds like a big undertaking'? Yeah, me too. If you clean your bike every month, it shouldn't get into such a state that a professional-standard deep clean is needed. Serious off-roading through mud, water and sand notwithstanding, your bike probably isn't going to get that dirty if you cycle recreationally and stick mainly to roads and cycle paths.

Give your bike a good clean with a bike or car shampoo or washing-up liquid diluted in a bucket of warm water. Use a cloth or a soft brush to scrub off any particularly stubborn stains. An old toothbrush is fine to clean your chain and gear hubs. Clean the wheels properly, using a small sponge or brush to get in between the spokes and clean off any oil or grease. Don't forget to clean your reflectors and lights. Then rinse the whole thing off thoroughly and dry with an old towel or soft cloth. Hey presto! Gleaming bicycle.

Once you've cleaned and dried your bike, oil or lubricate your chain (see pages 104–105) and you're all done. Remember to put some newspaper underneath when you're working on the chain to catch any stray drips.

Make life even easier for yourself by rinsing or wiping down your bike if you do happen to ride through any mud or slush. Dry it off thoroughly – don't leave it to stand and drip.

Servicing

Bike shops and mechanics offer a range of servicing options, from a simple check of brakes, gears and cables to a full strip-down and overhaul. Servicing is essential to keep your bike in full working order and to deal with any problems. At the very least, take your bike in for a basic service once a year. If you cycle regularly, cover long distances or have a particularly expensive bike that you are keen to maintain, have it serviced more often and more fully. Additionally, take your bike in the moment you notice any worn tyres or brake pads, loose or frayed cables, damaged wheels, clicking or other odd noises, slipping gears or any other signs that something is generally not right. For any emergency repairs, a bike shop is your first port of call.

The shelf life of your bike

With proper care and maintenance you will extend the shelf life of your bike, but nothing lasts forever. How long your bike will last depends upon a number of factors, including how often you cycle, how long your journeys are, how often you have your bike serviced and repaired, the terrain you cover and the quality of the bike in the first place. A good bike can last for many, many happy years. Many parts can be replaced and repaired. But as bikes get older, more and more repairs and replacements may be needed to keep it in working order.

Economically speaking, when it gets to the point when you are spending more on repairs and maintenance in a year than you would spend buying a brand new bike, it's probably time to think about replacing your old workhorse with a new model. An old, run-down bike can compromise your safety, if parts are falling off left, right and centre or fixings and fastenings are becoming worn and loose. Take advice from your bike shop or a mechanic. If they consider your bike to be unsafe, it's time to say goodbye.

If you check your bike regularly, keep it clean and keep your chain lubricated and tyres inflated, you should have minimal mechanical problems. The most common problems you will encounter are punctures, and you can deal with those yourself (see pages 107–110). The instructions and illustrations that follow will show you how. However, there is no substitute for actually watching somebody else first. Ask your local bike shop if they run demonstrations, look for a course in bike maintenance, ask a friend who cycles to show you the basics or embrace the internet and search for free video demonstrations of repairs.

Right: Rusting tyres and a grubby, dry chain means it's time to give your bike a good clean and oil.

Chain maintenance

The chain is the vital linchpin of your bicycle. Bicycle chains are strong and can withstand great amounts of pressure, but they need a bit of looking after.

Lubricating your chain regularly will keep it running smoothly. Without a regular drink of specialist bicycle lube or oil, your chain will dry up, rust and may eventually snap.

To lubricate your chain, you will need chain lubricant or oil. If you are working indoors, protect your carpet or floor by setting your bike on top of newspaper or an old cloth to catch any drips.

1 I find it easier to work on bikes when they are upside down. Find a soft surface that will not scratch or damage your bike, such as grass. If you're at home, put newspaper over a mat or old rug. Push your bell, lights and reflectors round underneath the handlebars. Then pick that baby up and turn it on its backside!

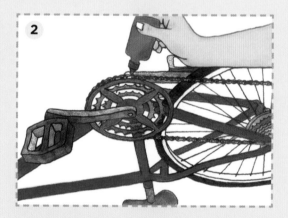

2 Lubricate along the chain and the front gear hub. To lubricate the chain, hold the nozzle of the bottle against the chain and gently squeeze a blob of oil onto the chain at the point where each link joins the next. Keep the bottle stationary and turn the pedals slowly with your other hand to move the chain along.

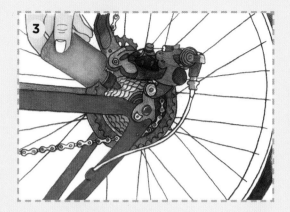

3 Pay close attention to the rear gear hub. This is where the chain works hardest, and the more gears your bike has, the harder it works going up and down the hub all day. Keep the hub well lubricated as well as the chain itself. If your bike has internal hub gears, ask at the cycle store for the best way to oil and maintain these.

5 Should you need to remove the chain from the rear hub, for example to change an inner tube on the back tyre (see page 108), firstly put the bike into its lowest gear, to put the chain as near to the edge of the rear hub as possible. Gently push the derailleur forwards and lift the chain away from the rear hub.

4 The derailleur is what moves your bike between gears and it has several moving parts. Oil it carefully to keep it clean. Shift up and down the gears and rotate the pedals a few times to make sure you have distributed the oil evenly.

6 To replace the chain after maintenenace, or should your chain ever come off the gear hub while cycling, you can simply lift it back onto the hub. Then turn the pedals a couple of revolutions with your hands to get things back running smoothly.

Tyres

The day some clever man or woman (my money's on a woman) invents a way to completely avoid punctures will be a very happy one. They are by far the most common problem cyclists encounter and I won't lie to you, they are a pain. I always find punctures come in spells as well – I'll go for ages without one, then get three in a week. You can't completely avoid punctures, but it's possible to minimize the risk.

Avoidance

Keep away from anything that looks like an overt puncture hazard. The most common causes of punctures are nails, broken glass and other sharp or pointy objects on the road. These nasty objects tend to collect at the side of the road, which is usually where cyclists can be found. Another good reason to cycle with confidence and claim your share of the road, and stay out of the gutter!

Choose an appropriate bike

Off-road tracks and paths can be full of pointy little thorns and twigs just dying to bury themselves in your inner tubes. If you cycle through a lot of rough, uneven, bumpy and rural terrain, minimize the risk by choosing a mountain bike or hybrid with thick, tough tyres that are harder to penetrate than thin, slick roadsters.

Stay inflated

Keep your tyres fully and properly inflated, and check regularly for any signs of wear. If your tyres are worn, they will offer less protection to the inner tube and be more prone to punctures. Check your tyres regularly for bits of glass, pointy and sharp objects or nails that may have become embedded in the treads.

Upgrade your tyres

Look into upgrading to puncture-resistant tyres, which are stocked at all good bike shops. Most entry-level bikes won't come with these fitted as standard. If new tyres are outside your budget, try a tyre liner made from puncture-resistant material.

Above: Punctures are most likely to strike when you are on the move – a good reason to learn to fix them yourself.

Use a sealant

You can also buy inner-tube sealant, or inner tubes that are already treated with a sealant. These will not avoid punctures altogether, but if you do pick up a small hole, the sealant can cleverly 'fix' the puncture from the inside by sealing over the hole.

When you find yourself struck down by the puncture fairy, you have two options: try and repair the puncture then and there, or simply replace the inner tube with a new one. If you're in a rush, go for the latter and you can take the old tube home with you to fix at your convenience.

Replacing an inner tube

To replace an inner tube, you will need your bike spanner if you don't have quick-release wheels (see below), a new inner tube, tyre levers and a pump.

The law of sod dictates that you'll probably be on the move when the puncture strikes, so push the bike to a safe place to carry out the work. If you're at home, put some newspaper down to catch any grubby bits that fall off the bike as you work, and have a cloth to hand to wipe your hands.

1 You will need to remove whichever wheel the punctured tyre is on to be able to change the inner tube. Before you do this, unhook the brakes.

If your bike has rim brakes, as most do, you can release the blocks by squeezing the top part of the mechanism together and unhooking the cable, as pictured. If you have disc brakes, follow the cable down to the middle of the wheel and unhook it.

2 Many modern bikes come with quick-release wheels. These feature a lever that you can pull towards you to immediately loosen the fastening. These levers may be fixed or removable. It is a good idea to keep removable levers on your keyring, so that you can screw them into place should you need to carry out any maintenance while you are out and about on your bike.

If you are working on the back wheel, you will need to unhook the chain first (see step 3). If you are working on the front wheel, go ahead now and open the quick-release lever by pulling it towards you, as pictured above, until it is at right angles to the fork (the bars holding the wheel in place). You will know you have opened it when you feel the wheel become slack and wobbly within the fastenings. Unscrew the nuts a little to allow the wheel to lift easily away from the forks.

If you don't have quick-release levers, get your handy little bike spanner out and unscrew the nut by hand until the wheel can easily come away from the forks. Lift the wheel away from the bike.

3 After you have unhooked the brakes, lift the chain away from the rear gear hub and take it completely off the hub (see page 105).

Use the quick-release lever or unscrew the nut using a bike spanner until the wheel is loose in its fixings, then lift the wheel away from the rear fork of the bike. Take care not to snag the chain – you may find it easier to hold the chain away from the hub with your free hand, as pictured above.

4 Deflate the inner tube if it is not already completely deflated. Unscrew the protective cap over the valve and push the pointy part of the valve. You will hear a 'whooosh' as the air escapes.

Next, use your levers to gently prise the tyre away from the wheel rim, as pictured below left. To do this, insert the flat part of the lever between the wheel rim and the tyre and pull the tyre away. Go all the way around on one side until that side is completely free of the rim. Either then pull the tyre gently off with your hands, or use a lever to prise the other side of the tyre away from the rim until you can completely remove the tyre.

Check the tyre thoroughly for the source of the puncture. Look outside and inside. You can run your fingers around the inside of the tyre, feeling for the cause of the problem, but be careful not to cut yourself. If you find anything, remove it.

Remove the inner tube from the wheel rim.

5 Unscrew the protective cap from the valve of the new inner tube and place this into the wheel rim. Replace the cap to hold the tube in place, as pictured above.

6 To replace the tyre, press one side of the tyre into the rim, using your hands. Once one side of the tyre is encased within the rim, begin to replace the other side, keeping the inner tube tucked inside the tyre as you go. Go as far as you can with your hands, then use your tyre lever to prise the remaining few inches into the rim. Take great care when using your lever not to nick the inner tube, as this can cause another immediate puncture! You might find it helpful to slightly inflate the inner tube so that it isn't so wide and floppy against the rim of the tyre.

Once the inner tyre is secure within the wheel rim, fully inflate the inner tube. Pump, pump, pump until you can't pump any more

7 Place the wheel back into position between the forks. Tighten the nuts manually with a spanner. To tighten a quick-release fastening, turn the screws for one or two rotations, then push the lever forwards, until it is parallel to the fork as opposed to at right angles. You should feel strong resistance as you push the final few centimeters and the wheel should be completely secure. If you can feel any give, or you can wobble the wheel, pull the quick-release lever towards you again so that it is at right angles to the fork, and turn a couple more rotations. Then push the lever back into place. Continue in this way until the wheel is completely secure.

If you are working on a rear wheel, replace the chain back on the rear hub and give the pedals a couple of turns to put the bike back into the gear you were using before you removed the wheel.

Finally, re-hook the brake. Give the tyre a spin and apply the brake to check you have re-hooked it properly.

There you have it! Problem solved and off you go. Pop the old inner tube in your bag and take it home to fix the puncture, if you have the time or inclination.

Fixing the puncture

To fix a puncture, you will need: your bike spanner if you don't have quick-release wheels, a pump, a puncture repair kit and tyre levers.

Remove the wheel, tyre and inner tube following the steps on pages 107–108.

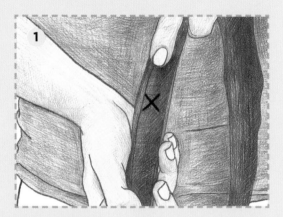

1 You now need to locate the actual puncture. Inflate the inner tube with your pump. Hold the inner tube to your ear, starting with the valve. Slowly turn the tube all the way around, listening carefully for the hissing noise that indicates air escaping. You may even be able to feel it against your cheek. Once you can hear the air, examine that part of the tube carefully to locate the puncture. If you find it, mark it with a cross using the chalk in your puncture repair kit.

Can't find the puncture? If you are at home or near somewhere where you can get your hands on a bowl and some water, you can submerge the tube in water and slowly work your way around. You should be able to see bubbles where the air is escaping. Mark the spot with the chalk contained within your puncture repair kit.

2 Your puncture repair kit will contain a small piece of sandpaper. Use this to gently sand the area around the puncture. Then use a clean, dry finger to apply a thin layer of the adhesive, contained within your kit, and leave to dry thoroughly. Do not be tempted to apply a patch while the adhesive is wet. It needs to be completely dry.

Choose a patch that will completely cover the area around the puncture. Remove the backing and carefully press the patch onto the inner tube, starting at the centre and pressing outwards with your thumbs or fingers. Be methodical and take your time. If you rush this stage, the patch may work loose. Peel any cellophane or topping off the patch.

Finally, pump your inner tube back up and listen carefully to the area around the patch for any escaping air. If all holds firm, replace the inner tube, tyre and wheel, re-hook the brakes as on page 109, and off you go!

If you can hear air escaping, remove the patch and try again, using a new patch if you prefer. There are some punctures that it's just not worth fixing. Large rips, multiple gaps or rips, or rips and tears around the valve usually mean it's bye bye inner tube.

Adjusting your saddle and handlebars

It's best to have your saddle and handlebars adjusted in the shop when you buy your bike so that it is all set up for you by a professional. But it is useful to know how to do this yourself in case somebody borrows your bike and adjusts the saddle and bars. Some cyclists like to remove the saddle and/or front wheel from their bikes when they leave them locked up in public places or at home, to deter thieves.

1 To adjust the handlebars, you will need an allen key and a screwdriver. Again, it's best to have your handlebars adjusted to the correct height in the stop, and you should not need to do so again.

Use the allen key to loosen the fixings of the stalk of the handlebars, located as pictured above. If there is a plastic cap, pop it off with the screwdriver. Re-tighten once you have adjusted the height and are comfortable.

The correct height for your handlebars depends upon your height, the length of your arms and the type of bike you have. As a general rule, unless you have a road bike, it's more comfortable to have your handlebars positioned so that your hands are higher than your backside on the saddle.

2 As with wheels, many modern bikes come with quick-release systems for adjusting saddles. Pull the lever away from the stem of the saddle to loosen the fastening, and push it back parallel to the stem to tighten.

If the saddle does not have a quick-release system, use a bike spanner to manually loosen the nuts, as pictured above.

Once you have adjusted the height of your saddle to a comfortable fit, tighten the fastenings until the saddle is completely secure. It should not twist in its holding at all.

When the saddle is at the right height for you, you should be able to touch the floor with both feet, but still feel comfortable on the pedals.

7

the
cycling
scene

This page: The hugely popular Skyride sees UK cities closed to traffic for the day to make way for cyclists.

You've bought a bike. You're all kitted out. You've braved the roads. You've fixed a puncture. You're a cyclist and proud. Now what?

Your cycling journey is only just beginning. Cycling can be more than just a hobby or a form of transport, or a way to lose a few pounds. For many it's a positive lifestyle choice.

The many, inherently brilliant credentials of cycling mean an entire scene has exploded into colourful, absorbing life. There are cycling clubs, cycling holidays, cycling races for all levels of ability, cycling fundraisers, cycling workshops, cycling socials, even entire cycling subcultures. The humble bicycle has provided artistic inspiration, raised countless sums for good causes and helped millions discover new friends, new activities and new ways of being. In its own intrinsically stylish two-wheeled way, the bicycle is changing the world.

Cycling and me

'I started cycling when I was 16 because my potential was spotted at school. The "talent team" came to my school and gave everybody a trial on the field. I passed and went through a few more tests before being given a bike and a coach.

I love the freedom and speed that I can experience. I get to travel the world and see so much more than if I wasn't riding. Cycling is my job but also my hobby. I have met so many of my friends through cycling. My greatest achievement is my silver medal in the Olympic Games road race.

I sometimes struggle when I have to do the base miles in the winter. I keep going because first of all it's my job but also because from experience I know that once I am out on my bike I will start to enjoy myself, and the feeling of guilt if I don't ride is no fun!

Cycling is fantastic all-round exercise. It can be very social and include stops at cafés or beauty spots. If you want to do it competitively, there is a fantastic domestic scene where you can enjoy the thrill of a crowd like we do!'

– Lizzie Armitstead, Olympic silver medallist, road race

This page: There's no better way to see the world than by bicycle.

What can you do on two wheels?

Getting involved in the cycling scene couldn't be easier, and you'll find it waiting to welcome you with open arms. Go ahead, get involved!

Join a club

A cycling club or group is a fantastic way to meet new people, make new friends and really revel in your shared interests. There are clubs and groups for all types of cycling. Have a search online for clubs and groups near you or for a local branch of a national club or cycling organization.

In many cities, the choice is endless. Fixed-wheel groups meet to swap fashion and art tips, cycle the city under cover of darkness and take part in longer or coastal trips in the summer months. Vintage cycling enthusiasts meet to appreciate the lost days of cycling. Many have their own beautifully restored penny farthings or other models dating back to simpler times. 'Tweed runs' see hundreds of vintage enthusiasts dress up in their finest garb and storm through cities and towns. Not to mention the hundreds of general interest cycling groups and clubs that organize events aimed at all ages, stages and levels of ability, from track days and open events to overnight rides to a far-flung destination. In the countryside, clubs may be devoted to exploring the beautiful natural scenery on two wheels, and may also run organized cycling trips into cities and towns to soak up the atmosphere.

Attend an event

On top of the events organized by cycling clubs, as bicycles grow in cachet and popularity, local and federal authorities, brands and charities are beginning to organize their own events.

In the UK, broadcaster Sky has thrown a great deal of time and money into cycling. Skyride events run around the country – these involve shutting off towns and cities to motorists for the day and letting cyclists enjoy the roads to themselves. Cycletta is a series of women-only cycling events, spearheaded by Victoria Pendleton, held at family-friendly venues around the country. Have a search online for cycling events near you, or try the Cycletta or Skyride websites to find your nearest event. Many charities including the Breast Cancer Campaign and the British Heart Foundation also run cycling events, such as the iconic and hugely popular London to Brighton ride.

In the US, there are also huge numbers of cycling events. Online cycling magazine *Cycle and Style* lists women-only events by state, including fundraisers. You can also find events listed on the USA Cycling website (www.usacycling.org) and at BikeRide.com.

Bike shops and brands are switching on to the soaring interest in women's cycling and many are starting to organize their own women-only in-store events. They can be a great way to meet new people and learn more about what's available in your area, as well as brush up on your bike-based know-how.

Go on a cycling trip or holiday

Bike trips are the new road trips. Forget cramming yourself into a car and crawling through traffic. Go on a bike trip. Set a route, rope in a friend or lover, stop somewhere lovely for lunch and devote the day to two-wheeled fun.

If you have a passion for travel, there's no better way to explore new destinations than by bike. A cycling holiday is a great way to get in shape and make the most of everything bike riding has to offer. Search for organized cycling holidays online or look for adventure destinations that offer cycling alongside other high-energy activities. If you are organizing a girls' getaway or a hen party, a cycling-themed trip or event can be a fantastic and memorable way to do something different and get everybody out into the great outdoors.

Lovers can hire tandems to take in breathtaking scenery on a bicycle that is literally made for two. Not that tandems are reserved just for couples – one of my best ever cycling experiences involved riding a tandem from London to Brighton overnight with a close friend. It was a little terrifying, completely hilarious and ultimately hugely rewarding.

Involve the whole family

Cycling is a brilliant way to get children into the great outdoors and help them burn off that relentless, endless energy. For toddlers, balance bikes are the perfect way to start, and you can enjoy hours of fun helping them learn to master their first bikes. Older children can learn to cycle independently very quickly and a family bike ride is one of the loveliest ways to spend a sunny (or even rainy) Sunday. Invest in cycling lessons for the whole family to instil valuable road sense into youngsters.

Family holidays to adventure destinations or resorts that offer cycling are a guaranteed hit with

Cycling and me

'The most memorable cycling event I attended was called the All Girls Alleycat, which was organized by the London Fixed Gear Forum. We dressed up as superheroes and followed a treasure hunt around London. All the pit stops were run by men dressed up as women. It was ridiculously good fun.' - Amy Fleuriot, fashion designer and founder of Cyclodelic

children, allowing them to discover BMXing, mountain biking or other more extreme forms of cycling that you personally might not feel brave enough for. If you do, embrace your inner daredevil and join in!

It's possible to cycle with a young baby, either by fitting a baby seat to your bike or investing in a trailer or carriage that can safely seat your precious cargo. Check the manufacturers' instructions very carefully, as these seats and trailers may not be suitable for babies under six months old. As always, do not do anything you don't feel comfortable with. Many mothers happily cycle with children in tow, but when it comes to your baby, only you know what level of risk you consider acceptable. If you don't want to cycle with your little one, treat cycling as valuable 'me time'. A precious hour snatched on your bike while a partner, parent, relative or friend watches over baby can be a wonderful way to recharge your batteries and rediscover your sense of self.

Embrace your silly side

Who said everything had to be serious? Cycling is a great way to embrace the fun side of life. Cycling clubs and groups often run events for the pure fun of it. The London to Brighton overnight ride my friend and I completed by tandem was not a charity fundraiser; it was just an event for people who fancied something different. There are hundreds of fun, irreverent events organized for two-wheeled fanatics and not all have to have a purpose or a serious side. Sometimes it's just about getting together to enjoy doing something different. As many of us cycled as children, getting back on a bike can be a fantastic way to give your inner child a bit of an outlet. Whether it's completing a bike ride or charity event in fancy dress or taking part in something totally new and different, cycling can empower you to try things you'd never have dreamed of before. Search online for events near you, or look up a local cycling group or club to see if they have anything special planned.

This page: Healthy, fun and affordable, cycling is the perfect family hobby.

Cycling disciplines

There are many distinct types of cycling, which sit separate to but alongside the overall cycling 'scene'. If you fancy getting into something a bit more technical, extreme or outdoorsy, one of the following might tempt you:

Mountain biking

Love getting down and dirty out there in the elements? So do mountain bikers, a down-to-earth, sporty, adrenaline-loving bunch. Mountain biking is one of the many cycling disciplines featured on the world's stage at the Olympics and it's a nail-biting, white-knuckle ride in which brave women (and men) take on the toughest courses on Earth on their trusty, two-wheeled steeds.

Mountain biking is for you if you love taking in tranquil country scenes, don't mind getting a bit mucky and want the thrill of extreme off-road conditions. For those with more modest ambitions, mountain biking is a fabulous way to discover new scenes and environments on dedicated courses and tracks, or simply to get around the great outdoors in a back-to-nature kinda way.

Get involved
Look up taster sessions at mountain-biking clubs. Try a cycling holiday, or go on a mountain-biking session at an outdoorsy family holiday retreat.

Get the look
Channel the outdoorsy vibe with simple layers. Think bright tanks and racer-backs teamed with shorts or a fun skirt (don't forget to pop shorts underneath) in the summer. In the cooler months, throw on a classic long-sleeved white t-shirt and go for longer, skater-girl shorts or water-resistant trousers. A weatherproof jacket is essential to fight those elements. Keep make-up to a minimum and go simple and low maintenance with your hair. You must wear a helmet for mountain biking, not only in case you take a tumble but also to protect you from a glancing blow from a low-hanging branch as you power through woodland tracks.

Road biking

Do you feel the need, the need for speed? So do road bikers, a tough, friendly bunch who embrace all the technological advances in the cycling world and love the feel of the wind in their helmets. Road bikers cover serious distances and take in all the sights and sounds the world has to offer while they're doing it. On the international stage, the road races at the Olympics provide compelling, gripping viewing. Anybody who watched Team GB's Lizzie Armitstead seize silver at the London 2012 Olympics in the road race or roared the US's Kristin Armstrong on to her second consecutive gold medal in the time trial will testify to the addictive nature of the spectacle.

The Tour de France is probably the most famous road race in the world, but women aren't allowed to compete in it and it has something of a dreadful record for banned substance use. Regardless, these, clean, days it's certainly a great watch for all cycling enthusiasts. There was once a women's Tour de France, but alas no longer.

Road biking is great for those who want to cover long distances, discover new places, have a hearty lunch and then glide off into the sunset in a companionable, friendly atmosphere.

Get involved
Join a local cycling club and get to know people who love the open road and a hearty lunch as much as you do. Go on a cycling holiday and enjoy your destination from the saddle of a sleek, speedy racer. Or look for organized events or races in your area. Many cycling clubs and groups put on events that welcome non-members.

Right: Get closer to nature with rough and ready mountain biking.

This page: Possibly the most daredevil of cycling disciplines, BMXing is cycling at its thrills-and-spills best.

Get the look

It's professional garb all the way for serious roadies. Go Lycra and proud. Sleek cycling tights, a colourful jersey and a streamlined helmet will see you blend in with the best of them. Show off those toned legs and be prepared to pick up a serious tan in the summer months – just don't forget your sunscreen.

BMXing

If you're into extreme action and shrug off cuts, bruises and broken bones as all part of the fun of testing yourself to the limit, BMXing is for you. BMXers possess breathtaking guts and skill, hurling themselves around courses of terrifying-looking obstacles on their tiny, bouncy little bikes. They also frequent skate parks where they can be observed pulling off incredible, gravity-defying stunts on the half-pipe and over ramps and other obstacles. Given the inherent risks of BMXing, it's very much a young person's sport.

Shanaze Reade is the UK poster girl of BMXing and has been hotly tipped for an Olympic medal for several years. Sadly, this has eluded her, but with her fearless, street style, she's become a role model for many young dare she-devils. In the USA, Arielle Martin and Alise Post fly the flag with characteristic guts, style and heaps of cool.

Get involved

You can hire BMXs from tracks and clubs to give it a whirl. Or go along to a skate park or race event and soak up the atmosphere to see if it's for you. BMXers tend to be a friendly bunch who encourage and support even total beginners.

Get the look

You'd be suicidal to even think about BMXing without donning the required full body armour first. You can hire all the padding and protection you need when you hire a bike. Away from the track, it's all skater-girl jeans or tiny hotpants, laid-back hoodies and super-tight vests and tees or even crop-tops to show off ripped, honed abs.

Track cycling

Enter the domain of Victoria Pendleton, Dani King, Laura Trott and Anna Mears – the velodrome. Track cycling is the pinnacle of super-swift technique combined with world-beating, cutting-edge technology. On the world's stage, there is no disputing that Great Britain absolutely dominates.

Speed is the name of the game here. Track cycling incorporates a series of thrilling and sometimes downright bizarre events including team pursuit, the keirin and the sprint.

Track cycling is for you if you're super-competitive and love to be the best, beat the competition and smash your own personal bests. The atmosphere within the velodrome is hard to beat. Training and racing will also give you an incredibly streamlined silhouette. It's very hard work, so you need to be prepared to commit, especially if you want to take it more seriously.

Get involved

Look for a local track, league or club and go along to a few events to get an idea of whether or not track cycling is for you. Many tracks will run taster days for beginners so you can give it a try yourself. Be warned – you might get hooked!

Get the look

On the track go for top-to-toe high-performance Lycra, futuristic helmets and serious leg muscles! Train in relaxed separates made from technical fabrics or natural bamboo for sweat-wicking, antibacterial properties. Cover up in sweat pants and a hoodie when you're not working up a sweat.

So there you have it. The cycling world is out there, all ready and waiting for you. All you have to do is join in.

Cycling and me 'After the Paralympic Games in Athens I did a bit of cross-training to stay fit and part of that involved going to the Manchester velodrome and learning how to ride on the track, as anyone can do. Then, in the early part of 2005, I picked up an ear infection. By the time I got to July 2005 I'd had six ear infections and each one had taken longer and longer to clear up.

I'd been using a bike to help me stay fit while I couldn't put my head in the water and during that time had completed my safety accreditation at the Velodrome in Manchester. I had also borrowed a road bike from British Cycling and had gradually been building up my confidence on two wheels. When I discovered I was banned from the water for up to three months I was gutted, but then British Cycling offered to trial me over 300 m to see whether I could meet the selection criteria for the 2005 European Championships. I turned up for the trial and turned out to be just two seconds outside the current world record!' – **Sarah Storey, Great Britain's most decorated Paralympian in history, with gold medals in swimming and cycling**

Embracing life on two wheels

Cycling is addictive. Don't be surprised if you find yourself surrendering to the cycling bug. It starts off slowly. You begin to find yourself thinking of ways you can cycle instead of walk, drive or take the train. After a while, you downright insist upon cycling. You're not interested in going at all unless you can use your bike.

Next, you start looking at your wardrobe in a completely different way. Although you still want to look great all the time, your first concern when buying anything new becomes 'Can I cycle in it? And if not, will it fit in my bag?' You may also find you have to start buying clothes in a smaller size.

Even your usual make-up routine has changed. Cycling has given you the confidence to go bare faced, or at the very least swap your usual base for a lighter tinted moisturizer. You find yourself embracing a more natural look, to better complement the glow in your cheeks.

I am afraid all of these side effects are very common among those infected with the cycling bug. There appears to be no antidote to the clearer skin, boundless energy, increased motivation, sense of fulfilment and beautifully toned thighs that regular cyclists suffer from. You will have to just grit your teeth and get on with it as best you can.

Despite the very addictive nature of cycling, it's not always easy to stay motivated. Even the most dedicated cyclists can struggle from time to time. This is especially true when it is dark, cold and wet outside and the thought of getting on your bike fills you with dread. You might even choose to take the bus or train that day – but don't be surprised if you end up regretting it and rushing back to your beloved bike the very next day.

If going out into the elements truly isn't for you, there's no shame in being a fair-weather cyclist.

Any cycling at all is better than no cycling. Plenty others feel the same way, as it's notable how many more cyclists appear on the roads in spring and summer! Come autumn, many choose to go back to the car or public transport until the winter is over – freeing the roads up for the hardcore who will cycle through anything. However, if you dress properly for the conditions, you might find that cycling in unpleasant weather is far less arduous than you imagined it would be. I always find cycling in rain, wind or snow gives me a huge sense of achievement. It's hard to beat that feeling of coming home a bit cold and wet and sinking straight into a lovely hot bath.

You may also find your commitment wavering if you are unlucky enough to have an accident, come off your bike or have a bad experience with a motorist. Such incidents can really knock your confidence and self-belief, particularly if you weren't the most confident cyclist to begin with. The best way to get back on track is to have a few lessons with a qualified cycling instructor. They can help you build up your confidence slowly and will show you the best way to handle such incidents in future. Even the most careful cyclist can learn a few new tricks to help them stay safe.

Ultimately, your motivation will come from the effect cycling has on your entire life. When you are keeping fit and active, saving money and having a great time while you're doing it, it just makes sense to keep going!

Well, that's it from me. Our journey together is at an end. But your personal cycling journey is just beginning. Hopefully, having read this far you are feeling motivated and inspired, and raring to leap aboard your bike. You should now have all the information and advice you need to sail off into the sunset aboard your two-wheeled steed. Stay safe, have fun and enjoy becoming part of the velorution. The cycling world is waiting for you with open arms.

Sources & stockists

Cycling holidays, events and adventures

Adventure Cycling Association
www.adventurecycling.org
America's bike travel experts.

Bike Events
www.bike-events.com
Organizes UK cycling events and holidays.

BikeRide.com
www.bikeride.com
Lists cycling events in the USA.

Breeze
www.goskyride.com/breeze/index
Bike rides for women in the UK.

Cycle America
www.cycleamerica.com
Bike tours.

Cycletta
www.cycletta.co.uk
UK cycling events for women, headed up by Victoria Pendleton.

Skyride
www.goskyride.com
Bike rides and events around the UK.

Cycling news and magazines

Bicycling Magazine
www.bicycling.com
US cycling magazine.

Cycling News
www.cyclingnews.com
Cycling magazine.

Cycle and Style
www.cycleandstyle.com
Online women's cycling magazine. Includes a list of women-only events in the US.

The Bird Wheel
www.thebirdwheel.com
US women's cycling site.

Cycling Weekly
www.cyclingweekly.co.uk
UK cycling magazine.

Sportsister
www.sportsister.com
UK women's sport magazine.

Spikes and Heels
www.spikesandheels.com
Fitness for badass women.

Official cycling organizations

USA Cycling
www.usacycling.org
Official cycling organization of the USA.

British Cycling
www.britishcycling.org.uk
Official cycling organization of the UK.

League of American Bicyclists
www.bikeleague.org
Advocacy and education for a bike friendly America.

CTC
www.ctc.org.uk
The UK's national cycling charity.

US Department of Transportation
www.dot.gov
Oversees federal transportation.

UK Department for Transport
www.dft.gov.uk
Oversees transport in the UK.

The Highway Code
www.gov.uk/highway-code
Road-use guidelines for UK cyclists.

Cycling fashion

Cyclechic
www.cyclechic.co.uk
Stylish blog and online store for women's cycling accessories.

Cyclodelic
www.cyclodelic.com
London-based cycling accessories label (ships worldwide).

Terry
www.terrybicycles.com
US women's cycling store.

Basil
www.basil.nl
Gorgeous cycling accessories from the Netherlands.

Bobbin
www.bobbinbicycles.co.uk
Classic bicycle and accessories brand.

Sawako Furuno
www.cyclefashion.co.uk
Cycling fashion, including must-have helmets.

YMX
www.ymxbyyellowman.com
US sports and cycling wear brand.

Sombrio
bike.sombriocartel.com
Super hip mountain biking gear.

Rapha
www.rapha.cc
High-end British performance road cycling wear.

Knog
www.knog.com.au
Super-cool bike accessories.

Vespertine
www.vespertinenyc.com
Safety wear meets couture.

Minx
www.minx-girl.com
Great one-stop shop for fashionable cycling gear and accessories.

Sweaty Betty
www.sweatybetty.com
Uber-chic high-end workout gear brand.

Velorution
www.velorution.com
Urban cycling heaven.

Wiggle
www.wiggle.co.uk
Tri-sports and bike shop.

Bike stores

Bike Shops in North America
https://itunes.apple.com/us/app/bike-shops
-north-america/id349824198?mt=8
Nifty app for finding bike shops in Canada and the USA.

Evans
www.evanscycles.com
Chain store selling everything bike.

Halfords
www.halfords.com
Chain store selling bicycle and automotive goods.

CycleSurgery
www.cyclesurgery.com
UK-based bike store chain.

Cycling training

Cyclinginstructor.com
www.cyclinginstructor.com
For cycle training, maintenance and repair courses in the UK.

Cycle Training UK
www.cycletraining.co.uk
Independent provider of UK cycle training.

League of American Bicyclists Bike Education
www.bikeleague.org/programs/education/
course_schedule.php
Find a cycling instructor in the USA.

Index

Acknowledgments

First and foremost a huge thank you to my amazing agent Isabel Atherton at Creative Authors. The journey always starts with you.

Thanks to my lovely editor Rebecca Woods, for 'getting it', for never giving up on it, and for her passion and enthusiasm for this project. Thank you to the team at RPS for their support.

Thank you to Dani King and Steve Fry at M2 Sports Management, Lizzie Armitstead and Andy Gouldson at MTC UK, Sarah Storey and Helen Scott at Team Storey Sport.

Big thanks to the very inspirational Muireann Carey-Campbell, aka Bangs and a Bun, at Spikes and Heels. Big thank you also to Jane Wake at Body-a-Wake for her input. Thank you to Cate Sevilla, Laura Hales and her pedaller, Lou Quarrell, 'Jules' and my army of lovely cycling ladies.

Huge thanks to Amy Fleuriot at Cyclodelic and Caz Nicklin at Cyclechic for opening my eyes to a world beyond Lycra and for all you have done for women like me.

Thanks also to Abby Burton at British Cycling.

Thank you to Simon Legg and the Friday Night Ride To The Coast team, from that silly girl who turned up with Rachael dressed in pink on the tandem.

Thanks to Rachael Wood, one of my biggest cycling inspirations.

Thank you to my darling mother, Fran Wallace. You are the only person I have ever met who never mastered riding a bike, but you made sure I did. Thanks Mum and Dad for the Raleigh Bianca, the Raleigh Amazon, the British Eagle Blitz and the Silver Arrow. Thank you to my brother Jamie for letting me nick your Raleigh Lizard, your Diamond Back Ascent and your custom-made mountain bike.

Thanks to my amazing husband Noel Bussey for getting me back on a bike, and for Pink Princess, Green Goddess and my Mother's Day bike.

Thank you to the incredible women of Team GB for a nail-biting, triumphant Summer of Sport.

About the author

Cathy Bussey is a freelance journalist and former deputy editor of *PR Week*. She has written several books, including *Brilliant PR*, and has made numerous radio and TV appearances. She lives in London with her husband, young daughter and two bikes.

Picture credits

Page 1 Mikkel Vang/taverneagency.com; **2** Cavan Images/Getty Images; **4–5** © Isaac Lane Koval/Corbis; **6** Cyclodelic (www.cyclodelic.co.uk), photographed by Andrea Vladova for Transport for London; **7** Cyclodelic (www.cyclodelic.co.uk), photographed by Farid Tejani; **8–9** photographs by Noel Bussey; **10** plainpicture/Johner; **12** Serge Kroughkoff © 2010 IPC Plus Syndication; **13 above** Dejan/Getty Images; **13 below** Mary Evans/Epic/Tallandier; **14** Popperfoto/Getty Images; **15 left** Cultura/Frank and Helena/Getty Images; **15 right** WireImage/Getty Images; **16** Popperfoto/Getty Images; **17** British Cycling; **20** © Martin Sundberg/Corbis; **22** © Sander de Wilde/Corbis; **23** Cyclodelic (www.cyclodelic.co.uk), photographed by Ben Broomfield (benbroomfield.com), model Claira Watson Parr; **24** Cyclodelic (www.cyclodelic.co.uk), photographed by Farid Tejani; **26** by 19 © 2010 IPC Plus Syndication; **27 left** Brompton Bicycle Ltd (www.brompton.co.uk); **27 right** Paul Massey/Livingetc/IPC+ Syndication; **28 left** © Corbis Bridge/Alamy; **28 right** Pashley Cycles (www.pashley.co.uk); **29** Pashley Cycles (www.pashley.co.uk); **30 left** R&D PHOTO/Getty Images; **30 right** Brompton Bicycle Ltd (www.brompton.co.uk); **31** Pashley Cycles (www.pashley.co.uk); **32 above** Pashley Cycles (www.pashley.co.uk); **32 below** © Rainer Jensen/dpa/Corbis; **35** © Mika/Corbis; **36** © Denkou Images/Alamy; **38** photograph taken by Chloe True; **39** Cyclodelic (www.cyclodelic.co.uk); **41** © Tabor Gus/Corbis; **42** helmet by Sawako Furuno (www.cyclefashion.co.uk), photograph courtesy of Liesel Böckl; **44** © Mika/Corbis; **46–48** illustrations by Qian Wu; **49** Getty Images; **50** Getty Images; **52** © Purcell-Holmes/Robert Harding World Imagery/Corbis; **53** helmet by Sawako Furuno (www.cyclefashion.co.uk), photograph courtesy of Liesel Böckl; **54** GUIZIOU Franck/Getty Images; **56** Andrew Watson / Getty Images; **57** photograph by Charlie Dark; **58** Ty Milford/Getty Images; **60** Brompton Bicycle Ltd (www.brompton.co.uk); **61** © Mika/Corbis; **63** by 19 © 2010 IPC Plus Syndication; **64** helmet by Sawako Furuno (www.cyclefashion.co.uk), photograph courtesy of Liesel Böckl; **67–68** Cyclodelic (www.cyclodelic.co.uk), photographed by Ben Broomfield (benbroomfield.com), model Claira Watson Parr; **69** the Isoar Wings vest by VESPERTINE (vespertinenyc.com), photograph by Reka Nyari; **70** © Philip Lee Harvey/Alamy; **72** © Ocean/Corbis; **73** Georgia Glynn-Smith; **74** Jane Wake; **75** © Pressmaster; **76–77** illustrations by Qian Wu; **78** Bowery Lane Bicycles (www.bowerylanebicycles.com) and Travis Huggett (www.travishuggett.com); **80** Jacopo Raule/Contributor/Getty Images; **81 above** AFP/Stringer/Getty Images; **81 below** Mat Szwajkos/Stringer/Getty Images; **83 above** Basil (www.basil.nl); **83 below** Cyclodelic (www.cyclodelic.co.uk); **84** Mike Lelliott for KNOG (www.knog.com.au); **85** The Trench, Oyster by VESPERTINE (vespertinenyc.com), photograph by A.J. Abucay; **87** © Corbis Flirt/Alamy; **88** Basil (www.basil.nl); **90** NBCU Photo Bank via Getty Images; **91** Handout/Handout/Getty Images; **92** © Joe Toth/BPI/Corbis; **95** © Image Source/Corbis; **96** fStop/Alamy; **98** Johner Images/Alamy; **101** Bowery Lane Bicycles (www.bowerylanebicycles.com) and Travis Huggett (www.travishuggett.com); **103** Tony Burns/Getty Images; **104–105** illustrations by Chloe True; **106** © J.P. Greenwood/Corbis; **107–111** illustrations by Qian Wu; **112** Wayne Tippetts/Rex Features; **114** © 2010 Getty Images; **115** © 2012 Jacopo Raule/Getty Images; **116** © Gil Giuglio/Hemis/Corbis; **119** photo by Søren Solkaer; **121** © Isaac Lane Koval/Corbis; **122** © Liang Qiang/Xinhua Press/Corbis; **125** Colin Cooke/taverneagency.com